If found, please return to:

_____

_____

_____

_____

INSIDE THE TEST KITCHEN

ALSO BY TYLER FLORENCE

Tyler Florence Fresh

Start Fresh

Tyler Florence Family Meal

Stirring the Pot

Dinner at My Place

Tyler's Ultimate

Eat This Book

Tyler Florence's Real Kitchen

BOOKS FOR CHILDREN (WITH CRAIG FRAZIER)

Tyler Makes Birthday Cake!

Tyler Makes Spaghetti!

Tyler Makes Pancakes!

INSIDE THE TEST KITCHEN

120 NEW RECIPES, PERFECTED

TYLER FLORENCE

CLARKSON POTTER/PUBLISHERS
NEW YORK

ACKNOWLEDGMENTS

Text and photographs copyright ©
2014 by Tyler Florence

All rights reserved.

Published in the United States by Clarkson
Potter/Publishers, an imprint of the Crown
Publishing Group, a division of Random
House LLC, a Penguin Random House
Company, New York.

www.crownpublishing.com

www.clarksonpotter.com

CLARKSON POTTER is a trademark and
POTTER with colophon is a registered
trademark of Random House LLC.

Library of Congress Cataloging-in-
Publication Data
Florence, Tyler.
    Inside the test kitchen: 120 new recipes
perfected / Tyler Florence. — First edition.
        pages cm
1. Cooking. 2. Food—Testing. I. Title.
    TX714.F6357   2014
    641.5—dc23   2013050639

ISBN 978-0-385-34455-5
Ebook ISBN 978-0-385-34456-2

Printed in China

10 9 8 7 6 5 4 3

First Edition

Hi, Francis!! I'm wrapping up FOOD TRUCKS in Fla. I just wanted to drop you a quick note and tell you how much I love the book. I think we killed it. #TFTestKitchen is in the can… thank you for editing it, man…

Right on, Tyler!

But you're not done yet… we still need the acknowledgments

I know my "creative process" is not for everybody, but a huge thanks to you and everyone at Clarkson Potter for going with the direction. The iPad-photos thing was cool, you have to admit…and the $1.99 photo toaster app that made them look like a 1977 issue of GOURMET.

The pleasure was all ours! Except maybe for sorting through the 48625 pictures.

Wait, are these the acknowledgments?

Yes… I'm texting them to you… just screen grab it.

Haha. There's this thing some people use called "email," but ok, I'll screen grab away.

I mean, this is book publishing we're talking about, so really you should be sending me a telegraph in Morse code or something.

Come on…I'm trying to say something nice here. My email is a black hole. No one in the real world knows how much work goes into a book and I've got to say I think this is the best team in the business. Jane Treuhaft and designer Laura Palese did an amazing job with the layout, and a big hug to Pam Krauss for hooking us up.

Yes, thank you! I'm so grateful to work with such incredible people every day. And please thank Alex and Tolan for saving our sanity throughout the project!

Yes…everyone on my team had it on lock. My wife, Tolan, Alexandria Dempsey, Donna Perreault… it's good to have people around to remind me I've been testing onion rings for 6 days and maybe it's time to move on. Erik Harrelson, our corporate chef, is killing it.

Haha, no doubt.

I couldn't be happier with the project. #TFTestKitchen is the new New—all about challenging what we know about cooking

Who else should we thank?

No brainer…everyone on Twitter and Instagram who have supplied the ideas and the feedback that made this book different and really interesting. It's 100% because of them. 20 years on television gives you a very tight support group. I love my people.

Definitely. Anyone else?

That's it… it's not an Oscar…

BOOK DESIGN
BY LAURA PALESE

COVER DESIGN
BY JIM MASSEY

FRONT COVER
PHOTOGRAPH BY
JOHN LEE

BACK COVER
PHOTOGRAPHS BY
TYLER FLORENCE

CONTENTS:

INTRODUCTION 8

- BARBECUE 13

- BURGERS & MEATLOAF 25

- CHEESE, FRESH CHEESE & CHEESECAKE 41

- CHICKEN & TURKEY 63

- EGGS & SOUFFLÉS 91

- THE FIVE-IN-ONE BAKING MIX 109

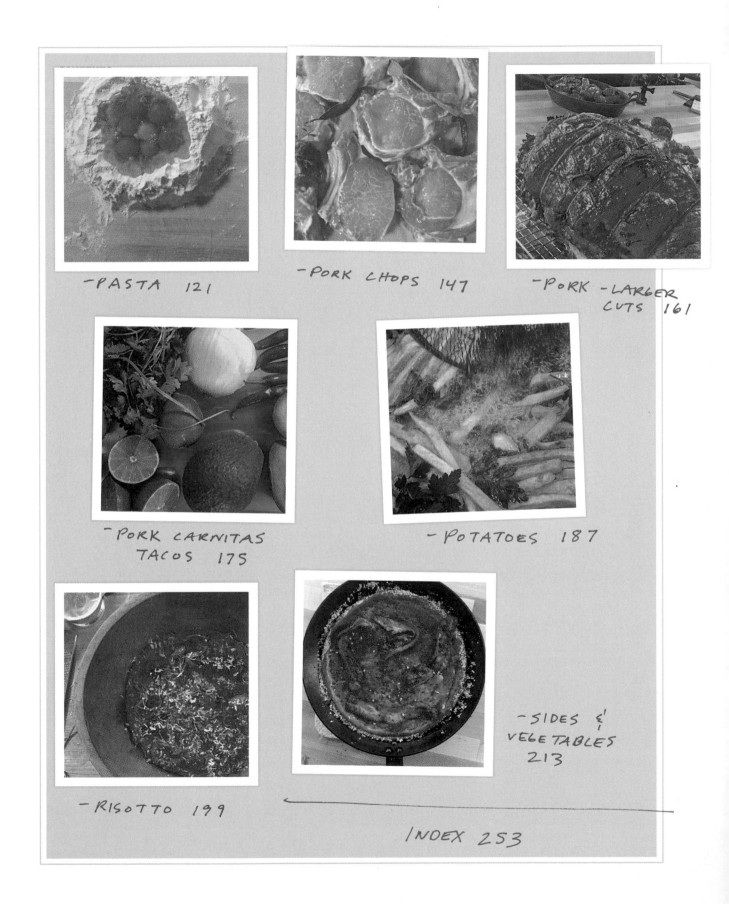

– PASTA 121

– PORK CHOPS 147

– PORK – LARGER CUTS 161

– PORK CARNITAS TACOS 175

– POTATOES 187

– RISOTTO 199

– SIDES & VEGETABLES 213

INDEX 253

I STARTED WORKING IN RESTAURANT KITCHENS WHEN I WAS FIFTEEN YEARS OLD, AS A DISHWASHER. I WORKED HARD, KNOWING IN MY HEART THAT WORLD WAS WHERE I BELONGED. AFTER A FEW YEARS, I WENT TO CULINARY SCHOOL AT JOHNSON & WALES UNIVERSITY, THEN MOVED TO NEW YORK CITY AND STARTED WORKING AGAIN IN THE RESTAURANT INDUSTRY — IN THE CITY THAT NEVER SLEEPS. I CAUGHT THE EYE OF A FEW TELEVISION PRODUCERS, AND SINCE THEN HAVE HAD A FORTUNATE AND FANTASTIC RUN, SHARING WHAT I KNOW AND LOVE WITH VIEWERS AROUND THE WORLD. I'VE BEEN COOKING FOR A LONG TIME — IN FACT, AT THIS POINT IN MY LIFE, I'VE SPENT MORE TIME IN THE ~~KITCHEN~~ FOOD WORLD THAN OUTSIDE OF IT.

Throughout those years, in all the places I traveled, with all the people I have cooked with and for, and in all the restaurants I've opened, I've always felt confident about my culinary knowledge. I've kept a firm grasp on my food philosophy: always let the ingredients tell their own truth, and they will deliver a high-definition experience. But I also think it's important to continue to strive to do things better.

One of the best ways to improve is to challenge what you already know. Why are we using the techniques our grandmothers used? Sometimes it's just because they work really well. My meatballs would not be as delicious as they are were it not for the Italian grandmother I worked with in Italy years ago. And my own grandmother taught me the basics of Southern hospitality; I always knew I would eat well in her kitchen, and I never left hungry—for food or for affection.

Other times, though, the old techniques and recipes could use a refresher. We don't have to tie ourselves down to what we already know: we have to innovate, push, go against the grain. We can't be afraid to take chances and to try again if the first attempts don't work.

THE TEST KITCHEN

In the idyllic setting of Mill Valley, in Marin County, California, is my Test Kitchen. Some might walk in and think it looks like a man cave: the leather-belt floors (they look like wood for a split second, until you realize what you are standing on), the buck's head on the wall, and the Marshall amplifier in the corner might make you think that. But it's really a center for culinary creativity, where me and my Test Kitchen team brainstormed, cooked, and tasted our way through this cookbook.

The door was always open, so there was a constant stream of visitors coming up from the restaurant or friends and family passing through town. The chefs in my restaurant El Paseo came up all the time, helping us refine the flavor combinations or taking notes on what we were doing, to bring them back down to their kitchen. I had a couple of friends from South Carolina who visited for a week, and they were firmly planted in the kitchen as well, tasting right along with the rest of us (though they all had beers in their hands). My good friend Jesse, who is a firefighter in Mill Valley, spent a number of days with us while he was recovering from surgery, and he gave us some suggestions on how to safely set up the Big Green Egg for our barbecue week.

I was lucky enough to have my wife, Tolan, around quite a bit, too—she is my go-to source for recipe questions. If she won't make it for dinner, there is a good chance no home cook will either. Also, my kids would pop by after school to hang out and grab a bite of whatever we were working on. (There is even a rumor that Dorothy, my five-year-old

NO BAD IDEAS
IN THE
TEST KITCHEN

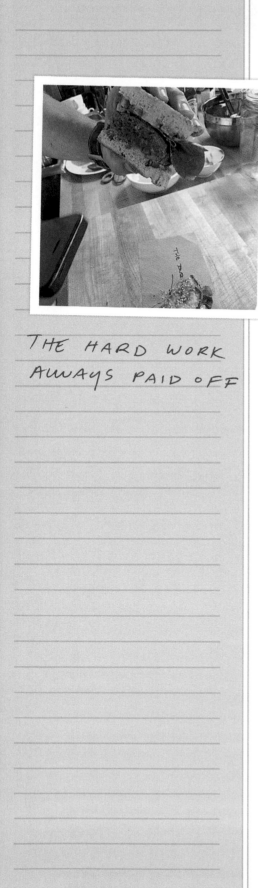

THE HARD WORK ALWAYS PAID OFF

daughter, has a crush on Erik, our corporate chef; she always seems to find a way to sit at the counter to "help" him cook.)

The environment was always high energy, and there were always forks readily available for wandering taste-testers. We kept a few markers around so visitors could sign the bathroom wall. We now have this great collection of signatures, drawings, and notes from everyone who passed through during the recipe development sessions—kind of a yearbook for the Test Kitchen.

We maintained a strict no-bad-ideas-in-the-Test-Kitchen rule, meaning that any idea put forth was thoughtfully considered. The only way to get through testing with a positive outlook (really, without losing our minds) is to have a can-do attitude. Even if something seemed impossible, we kept trying. Just because something hasn't been done in the past, that doesn't mean it can't be done right now, today. We had tests of endurance, of course: Just how many burgers can we eat before we land on the perfect combination? And there were mini-breakdowns: Erik may have tested enough mac and cheese to last him a lifetime, Alexandria nearly "lost it" during burger-bun testing, and I was "conveniently gone" for a few development days of the Five-in-One Mix (our all-natural version of boxed baking mix for pancakes, waffles, muffins, cakes, and cookies; page 111). In the end, though, we kept the faith that everything would work—and we now have an innovative and exciting new collection of recipes.

THE PROCESS

When it came time to plan the book, the first thing we had to do was figure out what to include in it. A few weeks earlier, I had thrown out a simple question to my Twitter and Instagram followers: What do you want to learn how to cook? And here's a shout-out to my followers: You are not a quiet group! You inspired me while asking for everything, from homemade bacon to pancakes to French onion soup. In truth, this book was born on social media. And the hashtag, #tftestkitchen, continues to grow.

Then it was time to write the list of prospective recipes on a whiteboard. I'm a visual person, and I like to see ideas written down or drawn out, so the whiteboard is an important tool in the Test Kitchen. Once we had the list, we put the recipes into buckets—breakfast, chicken, pasta, dessert, and so on. We took a step back and realized that these recipes already existed. So, why were so many people wondering how to make recipes that were already out there? Obviously recipes for pancakes already exist (I should know, I've written a few of them). There must be a missing link, something that people aren't getting in the other recipes.

That's when we knew this cookbook would have to be different. We would have to dive deep to discover what was missing from all those other recipes, and we would have to deliver those results, clearly and effectively.

We started each day by talking through a recipe to come up with a plan of action. What makes the best french fry? What is the pain involved in roasting a chicken? Why is yeast required in making bread? We took a step back to really consider what and how we were going to cook. We looked at techniques and recipes that had been around for ages, and we thought about how to make the ingredients really shine. We wanted to find a way to make each recipe the best possible, in the most time-efficient way.

One of the truly different aspects of this book is how we documented the dishes. I'm proud that we shot the whole project using an iPad. I wanted the intimate, real-time photography that we are all used to seeing these days on social media. Professional food photographers have made my food look amazing in the past. But *Inside the Test Kitchen* was going to be about *changing conventions*; and using an iPad allowed us to share with you how things really were as we were working. We were also able to "toast" the images so that they would look almost like those in *Gourmet* back in the 1970s. We were able to work quickly; everyone on the team took the photos you'll see in this book.

THE BASICS

Our goal for *Inside the Test Kitchen* was to empower you, the home cook, with the confidence to put even a simple dinner on the table. We wanted to equip you with the information that restaurant chefs have always had, but also information and methods that we were discovering for the first time, or even inventing. We tested these recipes repeatedly, unpacking each step to make sure it was crucial. And if a step didn't contribute significantly, we found a better way to achieve our goal.

We started with some basics. First, great food stems from quality organic ingredients—even better if it's local. I believe it is crucial to understand where your food comes from, and to respect it. Before developing our pork recipes, for instance, I called up my good friend David Evans, at Marin Sun Farms. They focus on 100 percent grass-fed, pasture-raised meat. David provided us with a whole pig for our testing, and we wanted to do it justice. That's why we came up with a unique brine that would make the pork taste even more like pork: We treated a pork chop like fine wine, identifying the complex flavors that were naturally present in the meat, and then developed a brine that reflected those flavors. That way, we would be enhancing all the hard work that

MY KIDS OFTEN LENT A HAND

ORGANIZED INGREDIENTS KEPT US MOVING

WE WERE
LUCKY TO HAVE
GREAT
CALIFORNIA
PRODUCE

David—and your pork farmers—have done, instead of masking it with competing flavors. The point was to let the natural flavors shine.

In fact, that general principle of letting the natural ingredients shine is what drove this entire cookbook. Seasonal, local produce and proteins taste better, and using them supports local purveyors. So, do shop locally as much as you can; you might be surprised at how much better your food starts to taste, right off the bat.

The other principle that governed our work was to take advantage of every opportunity to build flavor. For example, anytime you cook something in water, you are extracting the flavor from that food and then discarding that flavor when you pour the liquid down the drain. Instead, why not find a way to use or change that liquid so that the flavor is not wasted? Boil down the cooking liquids to concentrate their essences and use them for sauces, for instance. And we always tried to find different ways to use ingredients in the same dish, like garnishing a risotto made with carrot juice with raw carrot, or boiling corncobs to get more corn essence to put in a dish.

Keeping these basics in mind will help you take your cooking skills to a whole new level. The recipes here will show you how we did it in our Test Kitchen, and how you can do it at home. In fact, I hope you'll be inspired by this book to get started in new directions. I'd often ask the team if, perhaps, I was taking things too far—and, indeed, there were times when they pulled me back down to earth. But in the end, what drove our Test Kitchen efforts was an overriding philosophy: Never be afraid to try something new. Take a risk and see what happens, whether that means using a new ingredient or trying a new technique. We've put in the time on our end to make sure your efforts are worthwhile in these recipes, but when inspiration strikes, try out new ideas in your own test kitchens!

BARBECUE

There is something about a big barbecue spread that brings people together. I find that whenever I serve something family-style, whether the guests are related or not, everyone feels a real sense of community. Growing up in the South, I had hospitality coursing through my veins from an early age, and I quickly learned from my parents and grandparents that feeding other people delicious food is a guaranteed way into their hearts. Barbecue tends to be serious business, with some big-time regional rivalries. The dishes in this chapter reflect my Southern roots, and along with my current home in northern California, have allowed me to create something of a California BBQ hybrid.

While we were testing the meat for our barbecue chapter, we were inspired to come up with side dishes that would create a well-balanced plate and bring the flavors and textures you want with smoked meat, though they would be great just on their own. As for the meat, smoking the pork at a low temperature for hours makes it super-tender. And once the meat is in the smoker, most of your work is done, giving you time to prep the sides or spend some quality time with your family. To serve this barbecue, spread out the smoked shoulder and ribs on a big piece of butcher paper, which creates an informal vibe that will make everyone want to dig right in.

- CRISPY SMOKED PORK SHOULDER OR ST. LOUIS RIBS   15

- CAROLINA MUSTARD BARBECUE SAUCE   17

- CALIFORNIA DRY RUB   17

- PARKER HOUSE ROLLS WITH PARSLEY-GARLIC BUTTER   18

- GREEN GODDESS SHRED   20

- CALIFORNIA BAKED BEANS   21

- BREAD-AND-BUTTER PICKLES AND CHEESE   22

- BOURBON PEACH COBBLER   23

CRISPY SMOKED PORK SHOULDER OR ST. LOUIS RIBS

NOTES / INGREDIENTS / METHOD:

People all over the country are serious about barbecue: whether you're in Texas or South Carolina, you likely have a strong opinion about it. For me, it starts with quality meat. My good friends at Marin Sun Farms provided the pig, which led us to a whole week of sampling pork recipes in the Test Kitchen. We decided to smoke the shoulder, using inspiration from our roast chicken test (see page 69) to ensure a super-crispy skin. We found that adding the rub at the end prevented it from burning in the smoker, but brining ahead of time ensured deep flavor. If you can get St. Louis ribs with the skin on, we love to make them this way.

Our Carolina Mustard Barbecue Sauce gets its inspiration from what I saw growing up—instead of throwing away the drippings, we use them in a sauce.

A SQUEEZE OF LEMON BRIGHTENS UP THE RIBS

RECIPE CONTINUES

2 gallons Almond Milk Brine
    (page 150)
1 (14- to 18-pound) bone-in pork
    shoulder
3 tablespoons white vinegar
2 tablespoons sugar
1½ tablespoons baking soda
1 lemon
1 cup California Dry Rub (recipe
    opposite)

Carolina Mustard Barbecue Sauce
    (recipe follows)

Special equipment: smoker that
    will accommodate the pork
    shoulder (we used a Large
    Big Green Egg), wood chips
    (hickory, almond wood, or your
    choice)

Make the brine and allow it to cool down. Meanwhile, score the surface of the skin of the pork, using a clean box cutter or a very sharp knife, in diagonal slashes 1 inch apart. Be careful to score the skin well, but not to cut deep into the meat. Place the meat in the brine and let soak for at least 12 hours in the refrigerator.

Soak the wood chips in water for about 10 minutes. Light your smoker, setting it to 225°F. Set the meat on a rack in a sink or tub. Boil 5 cups of water and add the vinegar and sugar. Once water is boiling again, add the baking soda. Carefully pour the boiling liquid over the meat, concentrating on the skin. Pat the skin dry and discard the liquid.

Place a pan underneath the grill so you can gather the drippings from the meat. Place the meat on the grill directly above the pan, and smoke for 8 to 10 hours, until a thermometer reads 150°F and the meat is deep tan and feels firm to the touch.

Preheat the oven to broil. Transfer the meat to a sheet pan with the skin side up, and place on the middle rack under the broiling element. The skin will puff up under the heat, about 2 minutes.

Remove the meat from the oven and squeeze the lemon all over it, then season the meat with the dry rub. Slice the meat into large pieces, then chop small and serve with the barbecue sauce.

St. Louis Ribs: This is also a great method for skin- and belly-on St. Louis ribs. If you are using them, follow directions as above, but reduce the smoking time to about 4½ hours. The ribs are done when they pull apart easily.

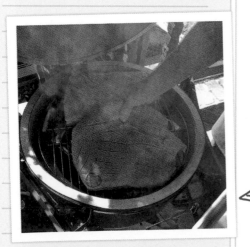

← I LOVE THE BIG GREEN EGG
FOR SMOKING PORK LIKE THIS

CAROLINA MUSTARD BARBECUE SAUCE

Makes about 1½ cups

¼ cup drippings from smoking the meat
½ cup French's mustard
¾ cup apple cider vinegar
5 tablespoons brown sugar

Add the drippings, mustard, vinegar, and brown sugar to a saucepan over medium-low heat. Whisk and heat until the sauce comes together.

CALIFORNIA DRY RUB

Makes about 2 cups

The herbs and the fennel in our barbecue dry rub make it distinctly California. We use it most by applying it *after* we cook the meat, so it doesn't burn to a crisp. A big squeeze of lemon when applying the rub adds a nice shot of acidity. You can also use this rub on chicken.

¼ cup coarse-ground black pepper (or peppercorns)
4 teaspoons coriander seeds
4 teaspoons fennel seeds
1 cup dried porcini mushrooms, or 1 tablespoon plus 1 teaspoon porcini powder
¼ cup kosher salt
¼ cup chili powder
4 teaspoons onion powder
4 teaspoons garlic powder
¼ cup brown sugar
2 teaspoons mustard powder
4 teaspoons sumac
4 marjoram sprigs
4 thyme sprigs
4 bay leaves

Toast the peppercorns (if using) and the coriander and fennel seeds in a saucepan over low heat. Once they are fragrant, remove from the heat. Grind the spices to a powder in a spice grinder or with a mortar and pestle. Transfer to a bowl. Grind the porcini into powder. Add the porcini powder to the spices, then add the salt, chili powder, onion powder, garlic powder, brown sugar, mustard powder, and sumac. Remove the leaves from the marjoram and thyme sprigs, and grind with the bay leaves to a finer texture. Add the herbs to the spices and combine. Keep in an airtight container.

THIS BBQ SAUCE BUILDS ON THE MEAT'S DRIPPINGS

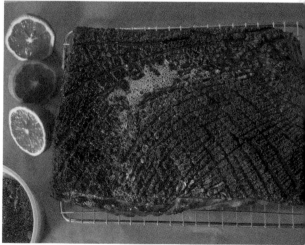

USE THIS SUPER-VERSATILE RUB ON CHICKEN, TOO

PARKER HOUSE ROLLS WITH PARSLEY-GARLIC BUTTER

NOTES / INGREDIENTS / METHOD:

It wouldn't be barbecue without something to sop up the sauce on your plate. Parker House rolls are a classic, but we give ours a Test Kitchen spin by adding a gush of herb butter to the junctions of the rolls right when they come out hot from the oven. When you pull them apart, you'll have some of the herb butter at each corner. These are fantastic for sandwiches with leftover barbecue the next day.

THIS GUSHING STEP IS A LOT OF FUN

ROLLS
1 cup whole milk
2½ teaspoons instant yeast
3 cups all-purpose flour
3 tablespoons sugar
1½ teaspoons salt
¼ cup potato flour (not potato starch)
3 tablespoons unsalted butter
1 large egg, beaten

4 tablespoons melted butter, for brushing on rolls

PARSLEY-GARLIC BUTTER
½ cup (1 stick) unsalted butter
½ bunch of parsley
4 garlic cloves
1 teaspoon salt
Freshly ground black pepper

Make the rolls Heat the milk to 110°F. Stir the yeast into the warm milk, and allow the yeast to activate for about 5 minutes, until frothy.

In a large bowl, mix the flour, sugar, salt, and potato flour. Melt the butter, and add to the bowl along with the egg. Mix well. After the yeast is activated, add to the bowl and mix.

Knead the dough together on a floured work surface for 10 minutes, until you get a smooth ball of dough. Place the dough in a bowl, cover with plastic wrap, and let rest in a warm place. Allow the dough to rise for 45 minutes to 1 hour, or until doubled in size.

Punch the dough down. Transfer to a floured work surface and cut halfway into the ball, then pull the two sides apart to form into logs. Cut the dough into portions about the size of a golf ball. To shape into rolls, hold a dough ball in your hand. With your other hand, pinch a far edge of the ball and pull it in toward the center of the ball that's facing you, and gently pinch it down. Rotate the ball about a sixth of a turn and repeat, until you have gone all the way around the ball and it looks a little bit like the knot of a balloon. Set the ball, knot side down, on the work surface. Cup your hand over it and gently roll it in a clockwise motion so that the knot tightens itself up. Repeat with all the remaining dough pieces.

Rub the bottom and sides of a large cast-iron pan with some of the melted butter, and place the dough balls in the pan, knot down, about ½ inch apart. Cover with a towel and rest for another hour, until the balls have doubled in size. About 20 minutes before the rising is done, preheat the oven to 350°F. Brush the risen rolls with the remaining melted butter. Bake the rolls for 20 to 25 minutes, until they are golden brown.

Make the parsley-garlic butter Add the butter, parsley, garlic, salt, and pepper to a blender and puree until smooth and soft. Transfer to a squeeze bottle. When the rolls are done and still hot, squeeze some of the parsley-garlic butter into the crevices of the rolls and serve.

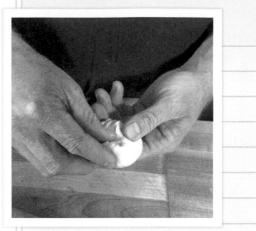

PINCH THE DOUGH TO CREATE A KNOT...

↰ THEN ROLL IT KNOT SIDE DOWN TO TIGHTEN THE BALL...

PLACE THE DOUGH IN A BUTTERED CAST-IRON PAN

GREEN GODDESS SHRED

SHRED THE LETTUCE THINLY, LIKE FOR SLAW

NOTES / INGREDIENTS / METHOD:

This is our version of coleslaw. You want a vegetable with all this meat, and the tangy, creamy dressing is an excellent match for the smoke and spice of the barbecue. Our dressing uses no avocado, instead relying on herbs for the color as did the original recipe from The Palace Hotel in San Francisco. Don't be afraid to let the dressing sit on the shredded lettuce for a bit; the texture gets really nice and tender.

DRESSING (MAKES 3 CUPS)
1 cup mayonnaise
1 cup sour cream
½ cup snipped fresh chives or finely minced green onions
½ cup minced parsley
2 tablespoons fresh lemon juice
2 tablespoons white wine vinegar
6 anchovy fillets, rinsed, patted dry, and minced
Kosher salt
Freshly ground black pepper

FOR SHRED
2 heads of romaine lettuce
½ white onion

Combine the mayonnaise, sour cream, chives, parsley, lemon juice, vinegar, and anchovies in a mixing bowl and stir well. Season with salt and pepper to taste.

Finely shred the lettuce and thinly slice the onion. Toss with the dressing. Let it sit for at least 30 minutes so the salad tenderizes, and serve with barbecue.

THE CREAMY DRESSING IS A GREAT MATCH FOR BBQ

CALIFORNIA BAKED BEANS

NOTES / INGREDIENTS / METHOD:

We love using chipotle chiles and Dijon mustard to make baked beans more interesting. The chipotles add a smoky flavor, while the Dijon-rosemary breadcrumbs here balance out the molasses and ketchup, and bring a nice crunch to the dish.

1½ pounds dried white beans (cannellini, navy, Great Northern, or similar)
4 teaspoons salt
1 cup molasses
1 cup ketchup
½ cup Dijon mustard
4 chipotle chiles in adobo (from 1 can)
Kosher salt

Freshly ground black pepper
Juice of ½ lemon
¼ cup California Dry Rub (page 17)

1 cup panko breadcrumbs
¼ cup Dijon mustard
2 rosemary sprigs
1½ tablespoons olive oil
4 strips of bacon

Soak the beans in 2 quarts of water and the salt for 4 hours or overnight. Drain the beans. Add to a large pot with 2 quarts of water, and bring the pot to a boil over high heat, then turn down to a simmer.

Combine the molasses, ketchup, mustard, and chiles in a blender and process until smooth. Season with salt and pepper and stir into the pot with the beans.

Cook the beans, partially covered, for 1 to 1½ hours, until they have absorbed the liquid and are tender. Check on them occasionally and stir. If the liquid is below the level of the beans before they're done, top off with a little more water.

Preheat the oven to 350°F.

BRING THESE BEANS TO ANY SUMMER COOKOUT

Add the lemon juice and dry rub to the beans, and season to taste with more salt and pepper. Mix the breadcrumbs and mustard in a small bowl. Strip the leaves from the rosemary sprigs and add to the bowl along with the olive oil. Mix well.

Transfer the beans to a baking dish and top with the strips of bacon, followed by the breadcrumbs. Bake for 20 to 25 minutes, until golden brown and the bacon is cooked.

007

BREAD-AND-BUTTER PICKLES AND CHEESE

MAKES 2 POUNDS OF PICKLES AND CHEESE

ICE BRINES KEEP PICKLES CRUNCHY

NOTES / INGREDIENTS / METHOD:

Cheese and pickles are a great combination, so we wondered: Why not pickle the cheese itself? To get super-crisp pickles, we used an ice-cube brine, which gets you pickles just about as soon as the ice melts. While we were pulling together the rest of the barbecue spread, we couldn't help sneaking a few bites of these . . . by the handful.

PICKLING SPICES
½ **teaspoon yellow mustard seeds**
½ **teaspoon brown mustard seeds**
½ **teaspoon coriander seeds**
½ **teaspoon black peppercorns**
½ **teaspoon dill seeds**
¼ **teaspoon fennel seeds**
¼ **teaspoon ground turmeric**
¼ **teaspoon allspice berries**
2 **whole cloves**
1 **bay leaf**

1 **chile de árbol, split in half**
3 **tablespoons salt**

PICKLES
1 **cup sugar**
1 **cup white vinegar**
1½ **pounds Kirby cucumbers**
¼ **white onion**
An 8-ounce block of Cheddar cheese
1 **pound ice cubes**

Combine all of the pickling spices in a medium bowl and mix well. Add the sugar and vinegar and whisk until dissolved.

Slice the cucumbers into ¼-inch-thick circles. Slice the onion into ¼-inch-wide slivers. Transfer the vegetables to a large bowl. Cut the cheese into bite-size cubes and add to the bowl.

Pour the pickling liquid over the vegetables and cheese, then add the ice cubes and stir. The ice keeps the vegetables crisp as they pickle. Allow the bowl to sit at room temperature. The pickles are ready to serve when the ice melts.

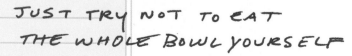

JUST TRY NOT TO EAT THE WHOLE BOWL YOURSELF

BOURBON PEACH COBBLER

NOTES / INGREDIENTS / METHOD:

Every great barbecue ends with a little something rustic and sweet. A good cobbler has a chewy dumpling-style texture, but done our favorite way, the bottom of the crust almost melts into the filling. A cobbler is an ideal way to use super-ripe fruit, so you could also substitute berries in this recipe when they are in season. Whether to peel the peaches is up to you. To peel them, cut an X into the skin opposite the stem and drop the fruit in boiling water for a few seconds—the skins will slide right off.

FRESH PEACHES IN THE SUMMER ARE ONE OF THE BEST FOODS

8 large peaches
¾ cup sugar, plus more for dusting
¼ cup bourbon
2 tablespoons cornstarch
1 teaspoon ground cinnamon
½ teaspoon kosher salt for crust, plus a pinch for peaches

1½ cups all-purpose flour
2 teaspoons baking powder
1 cup (2 sticks) cold unsalted butter, plus 1 tablespoon for pan
¾ cup heavy cream, plus more for brushing
1 quart vanilla bean ice cream or cream, whipped, for serving

Preheat the oven to 375°F. Cut the peaches into eighths, and put them in a large mixing bowl; you should have 6 to 8 cups' worth. Add ¼ cup sugar, the bourbon, cornstarch, cinnamon, and a pinch of salt, and mix well.

Mix the flour, baking powder, and ½ teaspoon salt in a medium bowl. Cut the cold butter into small pieces and add to the dry ingredients, cutting it into the flour with a pastry blender or a fork; you are looking for a coarse crumb texture. (Coating fat with flour allows it to stay suspended within the dough, creating air pockets that build flakiness as it bakes.) Add the cream and mix to get a sticky dough.

SEASONED PEACHES AND COBBLER DOUGH READY FOR ASSEMBLY

RECIPE CONTINUES

Add the remaining 1 tablespoon butter to a large cast-iron pan over medium heat. When the butter foams, add the peaches to cook and activate the cornstarch. Cook until the starch gels and the fruit juices start to thicken.

Assemble the cobbler by topping the peaches with tablespoon-size chunks of the dough. Push the dough down into the nooks and crannies of the peaches—as the cobbler bakes, some of the dough will melt into the fruit. Brush the top with a little heavy cream and place the pan on a baking sheet to catch any spillover, and place in the oven.

Bake for 30 minutes, until the top is browned and the fruit is bubbling. Let the cobbler cool down a bit before serving, and serve with the ice cream or whipped cream.

BOURBON PEACH COBBLER BEFORE AND AFTER BAKING. GRAB A SPOON!

BURGERS & MEATLOAF

Burgers and meatloaf. I'm sure you've seen recipes for these American classics hundreds of times. Trust me, so have I. But for the first time in my culinary career, the Test Kitchen has given me the room to dive deep and ask the questions that have bugged me for years: What exactly is the best cut of meat for a burger? What should go into a meatloaf so it tastes delicious both immediately and as leftovers the next day? I can now (proudly or not) say that I've tasted twelve burgers in one day, all in pursuit of the best version possible. It was an endurance sport, to say the least, but with Erik by my side as co-taster we made it through. Our testing led us to my new go-to burger recipe (see page 35).

Our Modern Burger Buns (page 28) was another test of endurance: just how many recipes would it take before we created a bun that can be made in about the same amount of time as the burger? We kept pursuing the idea, though, and eventually found a winning recipe with a whole new technique.

Everyone's family has a meatloaf recipe. (My wife, Tolan, makes an amazing turkey meatloaf that our kids absolutely love—so good, in fact, that it made it into *Family Meal*). For generations of cooks, *Joy of Cooking* has held a regal spot on the kitchen shelf. We wanted to come up with our own recipe—one we'd want to make over and over again—so we tested the tried-and-true recipe in that classic cookbook, and determined what we liked and where we saw room for improvement. I know you'll love what we came up with.

RECIPES:

- MODERN BURGER BUNS   28

- THE BURGER   35

- BURGER GOOD   36

- MEATLOAF WITH
     TOMATO RELISH   38

INSTANT BREAD ?

What's more disappointing than to get all ready for a great juicy burger, only to find out that you forgot to buy buns? That was a problem we wanted to make a thing of the past, so we set out to discover a way to make burger buns that didn't take hours for the dough to rise. Ideally, we wanted to make the buns in about the same amount of time as it took to make the burgers.

So, we asked ourselves: Why do we use yeast in bread? Its main purpose is to raise the dough: when yeast consumes the sugars in flour, it releases carbon dioxide, which puffs the dough up. So why not inject carbon dioxide directly into the dough? For years, we've loved playing with our iSi siphons. Like the squirtable whipped cream canisters you buy in the store, these siphons allow you to instantly aerate a sauce or puree by forcing compressed gas into it. We figured that we could make a batter that would be similar to a bread dough, aerate it using a siphon, and then shoot it out directly onto a griddle where we were also cooking the burgers.

We looked at the ingredients in English muffins, crumpets, potato buns, Parker House rolls, and traditional burger buns, and we tested them all with an iSi charger. We played with the ratios, exploring the time it took for the bubbles to form and the bread to come together when cooked on a griddle instead of in an oven. We knew it had to be possible. And not only possible, but also that it had to be great: with a texture somewhere between an English muffin and a Parker House roll, able to stand up to a burger's juices and any sauces, and also just the right size so it didn't steal the spotlight from the burger.

At first we had a lot of really dense biscuits; we learned that potato starch would make them lighter. Then some buns were too loose, coming out like pancakes, and some were too bubbly and just plain weird. Finally, we landed on the right formula: our delicious Modern Burger Buns (page 28).

MODERN BURGER BUNS

MAKES 6 BUNS

WHISK THE WET INGREDIENTS INTO THE DRY

THE iSi SIPHON ADDS CARBON DIOXIDE TO THE BREAD WITHOUT YEAST

NOTES / INGREDIENTS / METHOD:

This recipe was one of our big Test Kitchen triumphs—we wanted to be able to make a fresh-baked bun, from scratch, in about the same amount of time it takes to make the burgers themselves. It took a lot of testing, but we had faith it would come together. This bun cooks on the griddle, right next to your burger. The bun holds up well to the burger sauce and juices, which was one of our critical criteria for a great bun. There is no yeast required; instead, we inject carbon dioxide into the batter. Make sure you are using an iSi siphon that makes whipped cream, not a soda siphon. You will need CO_2 chargers, not the NO_2 chargers that come with the iSi gun, which you can get at specialty food stores or hardware stores. It's better to weigh the ingredients for accurate results, but you can also use cup measures if you don't have a scale.

9 ounces bread flour (2 cups minus 2 tablespoons)
18 ounces potato starch (4 cups)
2 teaspoons dry milk powder
4 teaspoons kosher salt
2 tablespoons sugar
2 teaspoons baking soda
4 teaspoons baking powder
2 large eggs, lightly beaten

Grapeseed or vegetable oil, for griddle
Sesame seeds
Flaky sea salt

Special equipment: iSi whipped cream siphon, 6 CO_2 chargers, 3 ring molds 3 inches wide and 2 inches tall, nonstick cooking spray

Combine the bread flour, potato starch, milk powder, salt, sugar, baking soda, and baking powder in a large bowl and whisk to combine. Fill a large measuring cup with 3 cups of water, add the eggs, whisk together, and pour the wet ingredients into the dry. Whisk to combine. Pour half the batter into the iSi siphon, and charge with 2 carbon dioxide (CO_2) cartridges. Give it a gentle shake, and let the batter rest for 10 minutes.

Heat a cast-iron griddle over medium-low heat and add a drizzle of grapeseed oil. When it's hot, lightly spray all of the ring molds with nonstick spray and set on the griddle. Eject the batter from the iSi gun into the ring molds. Cook for 20 minutes on one side, until browned on the bottom and the sides are set, then spray the bun top with nonstick spray and sprinkle with sesame seeds and sea salt. Using a spatula, carefully flip the buns and cook for one more minute, to brown the other sides.

While the buns are cooking, refill the siphon with the rest of the batter, charge with 2 more CO_2 cartridges, gently shake, and let rest for at least 10 minutes.

When the buns are done, allow them to cool for a few minutes. Gently run a knife around the edge of the ring molds to loosen and remove the buns. Spray the ring molds and repeat the cooking procedure as above with the second batch of batter. Allow the second batch to cool, and loosen as above. Slice in half and serve with burgers.

FILL THE RING MOLDS
WITH THE BATTER

A FROM-SCRATCH
BUN IN MINUTES

BUILDING A BETTER BURGER BLEND

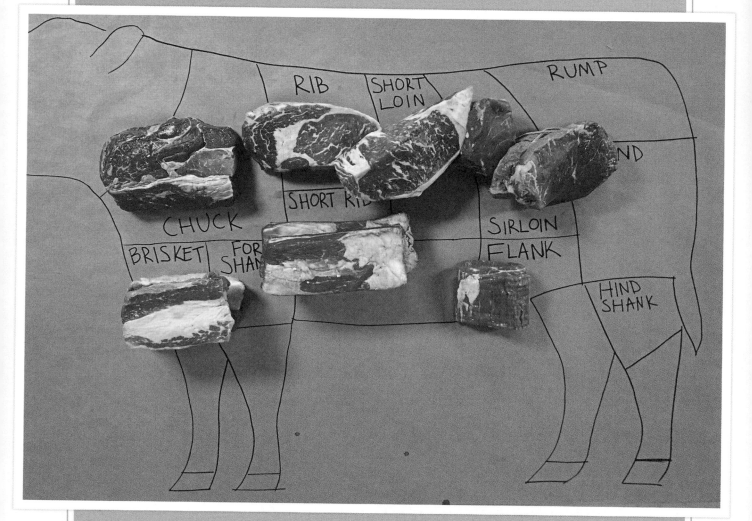

FIRST, WE CHOOSE FROM A VARIETY
OF CUTS, EACH WITH ITS OWN
CHARACTER.

FAT RATIO

80/20   75/25

70/30⁺

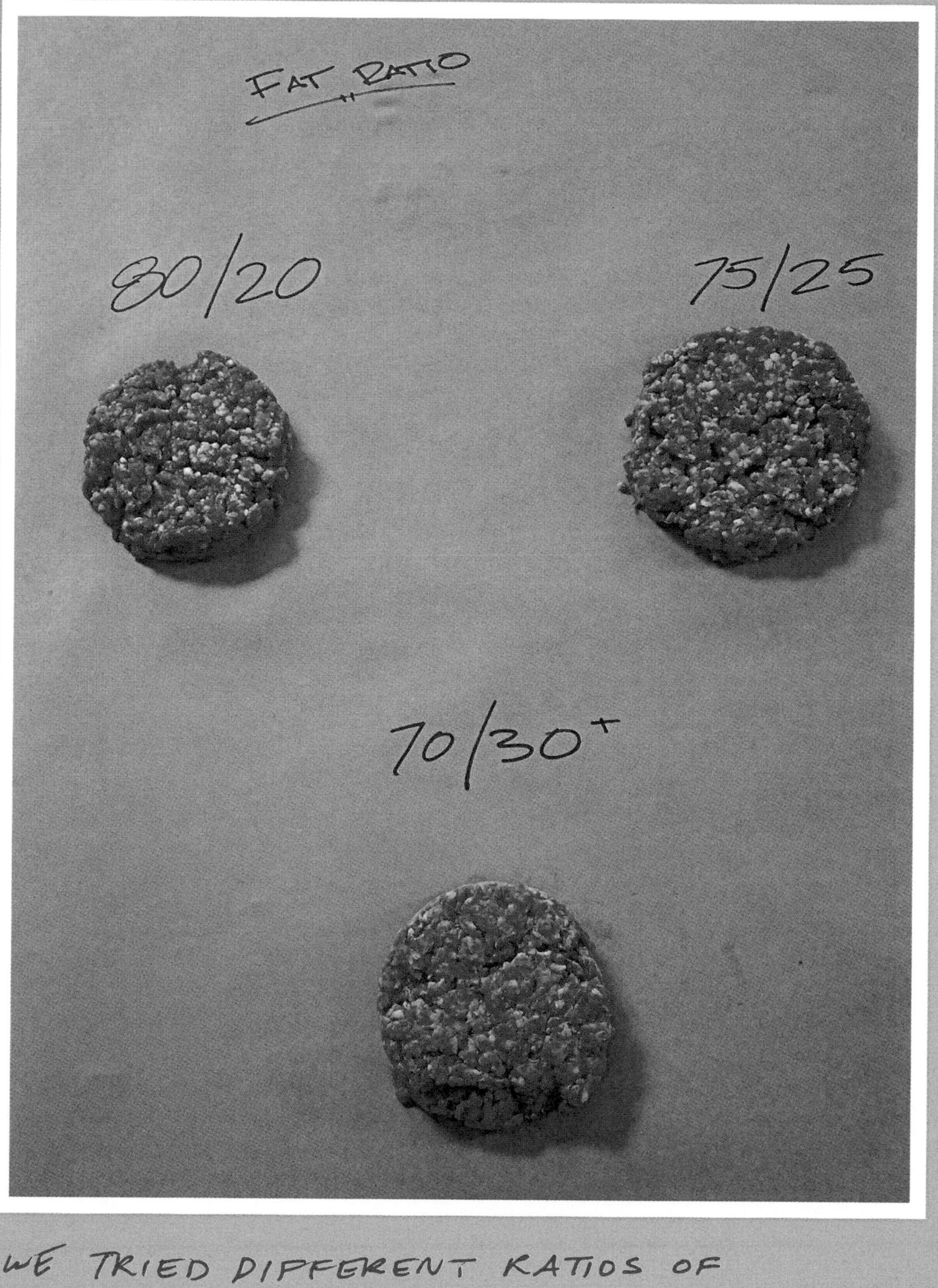

WE TRIED DIFFERENT RATIOS OF
FAT TO LEAN, FOR OPTIMAL JUICINESS.

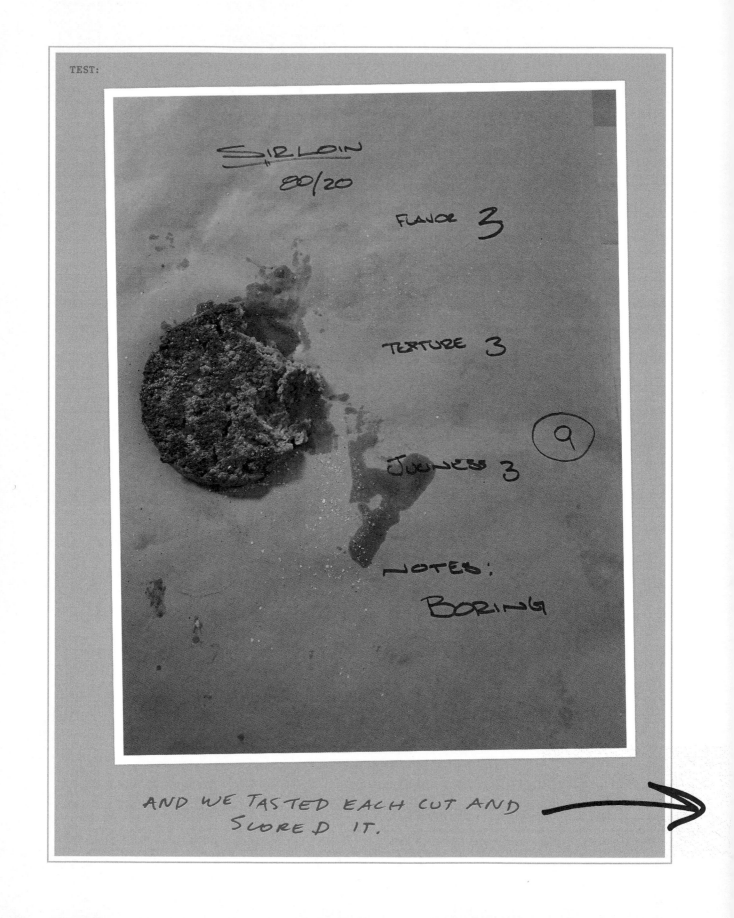

1 TO 1

Shortrib and Chuck

The Perfect Blend!

IN THE END, OUR FAVORITE WAS A 1:1 RATIO OF SHORT RIB AND CHUCK, IDEALLY AT A BLEND OF 75 PERCENT LEAN TO 25 PERCENT FAT. IT HITS EVERY NOTE OF FLAVOR, TEXTURE, AND JUICINESS YOU COULD EVER WANT FROM A BURGER.

THE BURGER

NOTES / INGREDIENTS / METHOD:

Don't wait for grilling season to make this—I actually like cooking burgers on a griddle or in a cast-iron pan better anyway; it gives a crispier crust, and none of the juices are lost through the slats. Besides, flare-ups from a grill impart a carbon flavor, not exactly a good taste for anyone. Shape your burger to be just slightly larger than the bun, so that after shrinking during the cooking process the burger and bun will be the same diameter. I also prefer burgers without too much stuff on them—I like a ratio of ¼ burger, ¼ bottom bun, ¼ top bun, and ¼ toppings. Let the burger itself be the star.

THE PERFECT BLEND OF SHORT RIB AND CHUCK

1 pound ground beef short rib
1 pound ground beef chuck
Grapeseed or vegetable oil, for griddle
Kosher salt
Freshly ground black pepper

4 Modern Burger Buns (page 28)
2 cups Burger Goop (recipe follows)
4 lettuce leaves
1 ripe tomato, sliced
French Fries (page 189; optional)

In a large bowl, gently mix the ground short rib and chuck. Take a quarter of the mixture and gently form into a patty slightly wider than the size of your buns. Repeat, forming 4 equal-size patties.

Heat a cast-iron pan or griddle until very hot over medium-high heat, and add the patties. If your pan is well-seasoned, there is no need to oil it, but if not, drizzle it with just a bit of the oil. Lightly drizzle the burgers with oil, then season them with salt and pepper. Cook about 4 minutes on each side for a medium-rare burger, then flip the burger and season again.

Carefully slice the buns in half. Spread the sauce on the bun bottoms, and place the patties on top. Top with the lettuce and tomato, and spread more sauce on the top bun and close the burgers. Serve immediately, with fries if desired.

RECIPE CONTINUES

IT'S ALL ABOUT THE RATIO WHEN IT COMES TO TOPPINGS.

BURGER GOOP

Makes about 2 cups sauce

This sauce is similar to Russian dressing, but we amp up the herbs and capers to give it some brine and freshness, so it contrasts perfectly with the burger. The recipe uses the same garlic aioli that we love with our French Fries (page 189), which you should make, too. Because what goes together better than a burger, fries, and some garlicky mayonnaise?

½ cup **Roasted Garlic Aioli** (page 190)
½ cup **ketchup**
¼ cup **Dijon mustard**
½ cup **Bread-and-Butter Pickles** (page 22)
3 tablespoons finely chopped capers

3 tablespoons finely chopped parsley
3 tablespoons finely chopped chives
Kosher salt
Freshly ground black pepper

MAKE THE SAUCE BEFORE YOU COOK THE BURGER

M.H.B. (MODERN HAMBURGER BUN)
LETTUCE
TOMATO
THE SHORTRIB/CHUCK BURGER 75/25%
THE GOOP

Add the aioli, ketchup, and Dijon mustard to a bowl and combine. Chop the pickles and add to the bowl along with the capers, parsley, and chives. Season to taste with salt and pepper.

THE JOY OF MEATLOAF

Meatloaf has never been the cool kid on the culinary block—and that's exactly its charm. Meatloaf is old-fashioned, classic, and reliable . . . and everyone's grandmother has her own version. So, we wanted to see what it would be like when made according to *Joy of Cooking*, the classic American culinary guide. Families around the country have relied on *Joy of Cooking* for decades to bring dinner to the table, but how tasty was this tried-and-true recipe?

We made this traditional meatloaf recipe and found areas for improvement. The taste of raw onion was overpowering, and it hid the flavor of the meat instead of allowing the meat to be the hero. Because we wanted to use beef and pork for what each brings to the loaf, there was no point in covering up their tastiness. Also, there was ketchup in the meatloaf itself, but we decided to bake the ketchup on top instead, for some caramelization and to concentrate its flavor. We added more salt to heighten the flavor profile and bring everything together. Taking these factors into account, we came up with a modern version that we think will become a new classic.

MEATLOAF WITH TOMATO RELISH

NOTES / INGREDIENTS / METHOD:

We found that eggs can make a meatloaf very dense, but using soaked bread in the mix keeps the loaf moist and irresistible, just like with meatballs (Spaghetti and Meatballs, page 138). Inspired by my dad, we made a tomato relish and mixed half of it into the meat. This packed the meatloaf with tomato, peppers, garlic, and herbs, giving it a great starting point, and then we carried that flavor through by coating the loaf in it before baking, too.

One of my favorite ways to make sauce is to take advantage of pan drippings; here, I simply blend the drippings with ketchup so as not to lose any of the meatloaf goodness. Use any leftover meatloaf in a sandwich—it's even better the next day.

MEATLOAF — SUCH A CLASSIC MEAL

TOMATO RELISH
Extra-virgin olive oil
1 onion, finely diced
2 garlic cloves, minced
2 bay leaves
2 red bell peppers, cored, seeded, and finely diced
Kosher salt
2 ripe tomatoes, halved, seeded, and finely diced
¼ cup chopped flat-leaf parsley
1 (12-ounce) bottle of ketchup
1 tablespoon Worcestershire sauce
Freshly ground black pepper

MEATLOAF
4 slices buttermilk or white bread, crusts removed
1 cup heavy cream

1½ pounds ground beef
1 pound ground pork
Kosher salt
Freshly ground black pepper

DRIPPINGS SAUCE
Reserved drippings from meatloaf pan
½ cup ketchup

SIDE SALAD
1 bunch of watercress
10 basil leaves, torn
¼ bunch of fresh dill, stems removed
4 radishes, shaved
½ fennel bulb, shaved
Shavings of Parmesan cheese

Preheat the oven to 350°F.

Make the relish Coat a large skillet with olive oil and place over medium heat. Sauté the onion, garlic, and bay leaves for a few minutes, until aromatic and starting to soften, to create a base flavor. Throw in the red peppers with a large pinch of salt, and cook until softened. Add the tomatoes (adding them at this point prevents them from disintegrating) and stir in the parsley, ketchup, and Worcestershire; season to taste with additional salt and pepper. Simmer the relish for 5 minutes to pull all the flavors together. Remove it from the heat; you should have about 4 cups of relish. Let it cool to room temperature.

Make the meatloaf Tear the bread into small pieces, place in a large bowl with the cream, and let the bread soak it up. Add the beef and pork, and half of the relish. Mix well and season generously with salt and pepper.

RECIPE CONTINUES

TOMATO RELISH IS THE SECRET TO THIS MEATLOAF

MAKE A CHANNEL IN THE MEATLOAF FOR THE RELISH

Place a piece of parchment paper on a sheet pan. Transfer the meatloaf mixture to the sheet pan. Using your hands, form it into a loaf about 5 inches wide and running the length of the sheet pan. (This provides more surface area for crust and makes it easier to slice and serve than baking it in a loaf pan.) Use the edge of your hand to make a long channel in the center of the loaf, and pour in the rest of the relish.

Bake the meatloaf for 1 to 1½ hours, until the juices run clear and the meat is tender—it should spring back lightly when pressed. (The internal temperature should be 155°F.) Remove the meatloaf from the oven and let it cool a bit before slicing.

Make the sauce Pour the drippings from the sheet pan into a blender—you should have about 1 cup. Add the ketchup. Blend until well incorporated and thickened.

Make the side salad Toss together the watercress, basil, dill, radishes, and fennel, then top with shavings of Parmesan, and serve alongside the meatloaf.

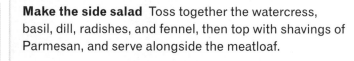

If you have leftovers, here's our favorite use for them.

Meatloaf-Avocado Sandwich (Makes 4 open-faced sandwiches)

4 slices buttermilk or white bread	1 ripe tomato, sliced
	1 Hass avocado, sliced
4 tablespoons leftover Drippings Sauce	8 basil leaves
4 butter lettuce leaves	½ white onion, sliced into rings
2 thick slices leftover meatloaf	Kosher salt
	Freshly ground black pepper

Toast the bread. Spread a tablespoon of sauce on each slice of bread, followed by a lettuce leaf and a slice of meatloaf. Top with a tomato slice, an avocado slice, 2 basil leaves, and a slice of white onion. Season with salt and pepper.

CHEESE, FRESH CHEESE & CHEESECAKE

"Cheese Week" in the Test Kitchen started with our trying to make our own cheese. We did a lot of research on the DNA of cheese, learning which are the good bacteria and which are bad, and how they behave in different environments. We went deeper, learning what effect temperature has on the results and exactly how specific varieties of cheese evolve. Our attempt at making our own aged cheese ended up, more than anything, increasing our respect for cheese makers. In truth, we killed our warm-weather-loving cheese by placing it in the refrigerator; let's just say that there's way more to learn about cheese making than we could fit into one chapter.

Fresh ricotta, however, is deliciously simple to make, and you get a super-sexy result that can be spread on toast or made into a gorgeous cheesecake. So we share that recipe here, along with stellar ideas for cheese accompaniments that will be standouts on any cheese plate.

Our stretch test was another highlight in the Test Kitchen. I had never really explored which cheeses were the stretchiest, but I knew that the big payoff in a grilled cheese sandwich or mac and cheese is the gooey, stretchy stuff. We lined up seven different cheeses to see which one would stretch the farthest, and the winner became our standard for these stretchy-cheese applications.

Baked mac and cheese is a favorite on menus at both Wayfare Tavern and El Paseo, and my kids love it, so I've also tasted my fair share of macaroni. Our Test Kitchen version has more cheese flavor—and more stretch—than any other that I've ever had.

RECIPES:

- MODERN GRILLED CHEESE 46
- STRETCHY MAC AND CHEESE 49
- SUPER-LIGHT CHEESE STRAWS 50
- CHEDDAR-BLACK PEPPER CRACKERS 52
- APRICOT-THYME PRESERVES 53
- FIG-HAZELNUT FRUIT "SALAMI" 54
- HOMEMADE FRESH RICOTTA 57
- SWEET AND SPICY PROSCIUTTO-RICOTTA TOASTS 58
- ICEBOX STRAWBERRY-RICOTTA CHEESCAKE BOMBE 61

TEST:

THE CHEESE - STRETCH CHAMPIONSHIP

What's the best part about mac and cheese or a toasty grilled cheese sandwich? To us, it's having the gooey cheese stretch out as you take a bite. But which cheese is the stretchiest? There was only one way to find out: melt and stretch batches of different cheeses. We tested eight varieties: Gouda, Swiss, Gruyère, jack, Cheddar, Fontal, Muenster, and mozzarella. We placed half-ounce cubes of each on a sheet tray in the oven at 500°F for three minutes, then scooped and dragged the cheeses across the sheet with a spoon. Gouda and Muenster were the two stretchiest in the trials, so we put them head-to-head for the finals. Muenster won the Stretchy Cheese Grand Championship!

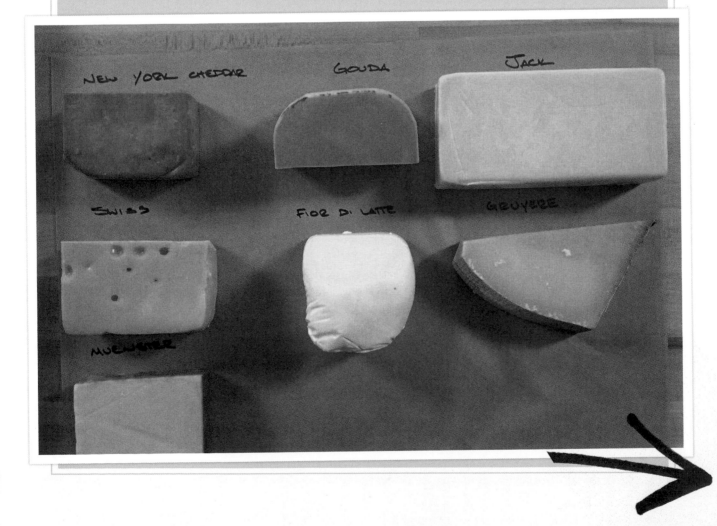

Stretchy Cheese
Grand Championship!
GOUDA vs. MUENSTER

ERIK AND ME TESTING WHETHER
GOUDA OR ~~THE~~ MUENSTER WOULD WIN

WE TESTED EIGHT CHEESES TO
FIND THE STRETCHIEST

013

MODERN GRILLED CHEESE

S

NOTES / INGREDIENTS / METHOD:

Somewhere between a savory Twinkie and a sandwich, our Modern Grilled Cheese uses the same batter and technique as the Modern Burger Buns (page 28). We cook the bread on the griddle at the same time as the cheese melts, creating something playful and indulgent. This grilled cheese is smaller than a typical sandwich, making it perfect for dipping into soup or eating as a snack; and you can layer on any additional ingredients you might want. As with the Modern Burger Buns, we recommend measuring by weight to get the most accurate amounts, but you can use cup measures if you do not have a scale.

A 12-ounce block of cheese (Muenster makes the stretchiest grilled cheese)
4½ ounces bread flour, by weight (1 cup minus 1 tablespoon)
9 ounces potato starch, by weight (2 cups)
1 teaspoon dry milk powder
2 teaspoons kosher salt
3 teaspoons sugar
1 teaspoon baking soda

2 teaspoons baking powder
¾ cup buttermilk
1 egg, lightly beaten
Clarified butter

Special equipment: iSi whipped cream siphon, 2 CO$_2$ chargers, rectangular molds measuring 2 inches tall, 5 inches long, and 2 inches wide, nonstick cooking spray

SHOOT THE BATTER INTO A RECTANGULAR MOLD

Cut the cheese into ten ½-inch-wide sticks about 4 inches long.

Place the bread flour, potato starch, milk powder, salt, sugar, baking soda, and baking powder in a large bowl and whisk to combine. Fill a large measuring cup with ¾ cup water, the buttermilk, and egg, and lightly beat. Pour the wet ingredients into the dry, and whisk to combine. Pour the batter into an iSi gun, and charge with 2 cartridges. Let the batter rest for 10 minutes.

Heat a cast-iron griddle to medium-low and add a tablespoon of clarified butter to the griddle. Lightly spray the molds with nonstick spray and set on the griddle.

Eject the batter from the iSi gun into the molds, just covering the base. Top with a stick of cheese, then eject more of the batter onto the cheese, just covering the top. You will end up with a grilled cheese stick about 1 inch tall.

Cook for 4 minutes on one side, or until it is golden brown, puffed, and set. Use a spatula to carefully flip and cook for 2 or 3 minutes more to brown the other side. Remove from the griddle and serve immediately.

Bacon Grilled Cheese: Place a piece of bacon on the griddle within the rectangular mold and cook until just crisp. Eject a layer of the batter on top of the bacon, followed by a piece of the cheese, then another layer of the batter. Cook as above.

Mushroom Grilled Cheese: Place slices of fresh mushrooms (chanterelles are great) on the griddle, and drizzle with clarified butter. Once they have cooked, season with salt and place them in the rectangular mold. Eject a layer of the batter on top, followed by a stick of cheese and some caramelized onions, then another layer of batter. Grate fresh garlic over the top layer, and cook as above. (To caramelize onions: Heat 1 tablespoon olive oil and 1 tablespoon butter in a large saucepan over medium heat. Add 2 thinly sliced onions and season with salt and pepper. Turn the heat down to low and cook until well caramelized, stirring, about 20 minutes.)

USE MUENSTER CHEESE FOR A CRAZY-STRETCHY RESULT

STRETCHY MAC AND CHEESE

NOTES / INGREDIENTS / METHOD:

Our goal here was to have a cheesy, stretchy macaroni and cheese that we could also make without a long baking time. We used Muenster, since it won our cheese stretch test. But after testing multiple versions, we learned that to make a really stretchy, cheesy mac and cheese, you want to fold cubes of cheese into the pasta—instead of grating the cheese into the sauce—then flash-broil it just to melt the cheese and crisp the breadcrumbs. This is the most satisfying mac and cheese any of us have had in a long time.

¼ cup (½ stick) unsalted butter
¼ cup all-purpose flour
2 cups heavy cream
2 cups whole milk
2 garlic cloves, smashed
5 thyme sprigs
2 bay leaves
1 pound dry pasta, such as elbow macaroni

2 teaspoons salt
½ teaspoon freshly ground black pepper
1 pound Muenster, cut into ½-inch cubes (or Gouda or jack)
⅓ cup panko breadcrumbs
Smoked olive oil or extra-virgin olive oil
2 tablespoons chopped chives

Preheat the oven to broil and set a large pasta pot of heavily salted water over high heat to come to a boil.

Melt the butter in a large pot over medium heat. Add the flour to make a roux, stirring well so that it cooks evenly and turns golden blond. Whisk in the cream and milk a little bit at a time, so there are no lumps. Add the garlic, along with the whole sprigs of thyme and the bay leaves. Stir to make a béchamel. Simmer over medium heat, stirring occasionally to prevent the bottom of the pot from scorching, until it thickens, about 10 minutes. Season the béchamel with salt and pepper.

Cook the pasta in the boiling water according to the package directions. Drain.

Mix the béchamel with the cooked pasta. Immediately add the cheese and mix well, so that the heat and motion melt and stretch the cheese. Transfer to a baking dish and top with the breadcrumbs.

Broil on a lower rack of the oven for about 5 minutes, or until the breadcrumbs are golden brown. Drizzle with olive oil and sprinkle with the chives.

MAKE A GOLDEN BLOND ROUX

FOLD CUBES OF MUENSTER INTO THE PASTA

015

SUPER-LIGHT CHEESE STRAWS

MAKES 10 STRAWS

YOU'LL MAKE A GOUGÈRE BATTER AS THE BASE

NOTES / INGREDIENTS / METHOD:

Gougères are airy French cheese puffs, but by piping them into long lines, we found that they bake up as super-light cheese straws. Then we amped them up with herbs, sea salt, bacon, and more cheese. The toppings bring interesting textures and pops of flavor as you eat the straws. These are great to have on hand for a party, or just to snack on.

½ cup water
½ cup whole milk
½ cup (1 stick) unsalted butter
1 teaspoon salt
½ teaspoon sugar
1 cup all-purpose flour
4 large eggs
1 cup grated Gruyère cheese
Extra-virgin olive oil

TOPPINGS (OPTIONAL)
2 slices of bacon
1 thyme sprig
1 rosemary sprig
1 teaspoon fennel seeds
Coarse sea salt
Freshly ground black pepper

Preheat the oven to 425°F. In a medium pot, combine the water, milk, butter, salt, and sugar and set over medium-high heat. Once the milk boils and the butter has melted, take the pot off the heat and add the flour all at once, stirring with a wooden spoon. Place the pot back over the heat and beat the dough vigorously for 2 minutes, until the dough pulls away from the sides of the pot. Let the mixture cool down for a minute.

With the spoon, beat the eggs into the batter one at a time, mixing until each egg is totally incorporated before adding the next. Beat in ¾ cup of the cheese, reserving ¼ cup for sprinkling on at the end.

Transfer the batter to a large pastry bag, or a large zipper plastic bag. Make sure the batter is pushed toward the bottom of the bag. Cut the tip of the bag with scissors so you have an opening about the size of a pencil. Squeeze long lines of the batter about 1 inch apart onto a parchment-lined baking sheet. Brush the straws with olive oil.

Prepare the toppings (use any or all of them) Mince and crisp the bacon in a pan, and drain on paper towel. Remove the leaves from the herb sprigs. Generously add the toppings to the cheese straws as desired, being sure to season with salt and pepper and sprinkle on the remaining ¼ cup of the Gruyère.

Bake the cheese straws in the oven for about 20 minutes, until golden brown. Serve immediately, or let cool and keep in an airtight container for up to 3 days.

AN IMPRESSIVE BUT EASY SNACK FOR YOUR NEXT PARTY

ADD THE TOPPINGS YOU WANT

016 CHEDDAR–BLACK PEPPER CRACKERS

4 to 6
AS A SNACK

NOTES / INGREDIENTS / METHOD:

Cheese crackers are delicious, whether you're a little kid, a college student, or an adult. We made ours special by adding a ton of black pepper and baking them as one large sheet so they can break into big, dramatic shards. These are great on their own, but they're especially good with the sweet-savory Apricot-Thyme Preserves (opposite).

THE DOUGH WILL JUST COME TOGETHER

½ cup shredded sharp Cheddar cheese

¾ cup all-purpose flour

1 teaspoon kosher salt

1 teaspoon freshly ground black pepper

4 tablespoons (½ stick) unsalted butter, cold and diced

Coarse sea salt

Preheat the oven to 375°F. Place the cheese, flour, salt, and pepper in a food processor and mix well. Add the butter and pulse until the mixture is the size of peas. With the processor on, drizzle in 2 tablespoons water, 1 tablespoon at a time, through the opening in the lid. The dough will come together.

Transfer the dough to a piece of parchment on a flat surface. Place another piece of parchment on top of the dough, and roll out the dough until about ¼ inch thick.

Pull the bottom sheet of parchment paper with the dough onto a baking sheet, and bake for 25 minutes, until golden brown throughout. Sprinkle with sea salt. Let the cracker sheet cool. Break it into large pieces with your hands. Arrange on a plate and serve alongside the preserves.

ROLL OUT THE DOUGH ON A SHEET OF PARCHMENT

APRICOT-THYME PRESERVES

MAKES ABOUT 2 CUPS

017

NOTES / INGREDIENTS / METHOD:

The balance of sweet and savory in these preserves makes them a flexible accompaniment for a cheese platter—or a spread on Cheddar Black-Pepper Crackers (opposite).

12 ounces dried apricots
¾ cup white wine
⅓ cup apple cider vinegar
⅓ cup sugar

½ teaspoon salt
¼ teaspoon juniper berries
2 thyme sprigs
Chile oil (optional)

Add the apricots, wine, vinegar, ⅓ cup water, the sugar, salt, juniper berries, and thyme to a medium saucepan over medium heat. Bring to a boil, then reduce to a gentle simmer. Cook until thick and most of the liquid has evaporated, about 20 minutes. Drizzle with chile oil, if desired.

THESE PRESERVES ARE GREAT WITH CHEESE

FIG-HAZELNUT FRUIT "SALAMI"

CHOP THE FIGS AND HAZELNUTS IN A FOOD PROCESSOR

NOTES / INGREDIENTS / METHOD:

Dried fruits and nuts are both typically found on a cheese plate, but in the Test Kitchen we aren't usually a crowd that sticks to the typical. We wanted to make a "salami" out of dried fruit and nuts, and we chose dried Mission figs to give this a California twist. It's chewy, sweet, and complex—and it's a cool presentation. Once the salami is formed, serve it with cheese or enjoy a bite with a glass of dessert wine.

¼ cup dry-roasted hazelnuts
10 ounces dried Black Mission figs
Pinch of ground cinnamon

Pinch of ground cardamom
1 teaspoon salt

Place the hazelnuts in a food processor and chop until fine, but leave some bigger pieces for texture. Remove from the processor.

Remove any stems from the dried figs and add the figs to the food processor. Pour in a splash of water to loosen the figs, and process until you have a paste that just comes together when pinched. Put the nuts back in the processor with the figs and add the cinnamon, cardamom, and salt; mix to combine.

Transfer the mixture to a sheet of parchment paper on a counter. Using the parchment to shape the mixture, gently squeeze it into a log and roll it. Then, form a circle with your thumb and index finger and smooth the salami by running your finger "circle" along the length of the log. Repeat, alternating these steps, until you have a consistently smooth and even salami.

Roll the parchment paper around the salami, then twist the ends tightly like a candy wrapper to secure the shape. Unwrap the log and place on a drying rack on the counter for around 4 hours, until dry to the touch.

Slice thin and serve the slices with any soft cheese; store leftovers in an airtight container.

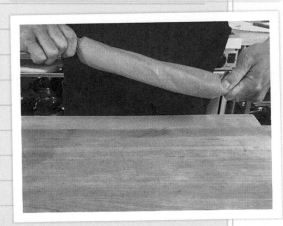

TWIST THE ENDS OF THE PARCHMENT LIKE A CANDY WRAPPER

HOMEMADE FRESH RICOTTA

makes about 3 cups

NOTES / INGREDIENTS / METHOD:

In Italian, *ricotta* means "cooked twice," since it is usually made from whey that's left over from another cheese-making process. Here, we use fresh whole milk and curdle it with acid. We like using lemon juice because it adds a sweetness and soft aroma you wouldn't get with vinegar. Rennet is great for other cheese-making applications, but not here, as it requires you to acidify the milk, which takes at least 8 hours; our version can be done in as little as 3 hours.

Fresh ricotta will last up to a week in an airtight container in the refrigerator. Save the whey, too, since it's a great cooking liquid for beans or meats, or if you're making the Icebox Strawberry-Ricotta Cheesecake Bombe (page 61).

4 quarts whole milk
1 quart heavy cream

¾ cup lemon juice (from about 4 lemons)

ADD THE LEMON JUICE TO THE HOT MILK

In a large pot with a thermometer, bring the milk and cream up to 180°F over medium heat. Stir as the milk heats to prevent burning on the bottom.

Meanwhile, strain the lemon juice if necessary to remove any seeds or pulp.

Turn the heat off, add the lemon juice to the hot milk, and stir gently for 2 minutes. Then let the milk sit for 10 minutes, untouched, to allow it to curdle.

Line a deep strainer with a few layers of cheesecloth and set it over a large container. Carefully pour the curdled milk into the strainer; it may work best to ladle it in gently. Let the whey drain from the curds for at least 3 hours. The longer you let it drain, the firmer the texture will be; if you'd like to let it drain for longer than 3 hours, place it in the refrigerator.

USE THE RICOTTA FOR CHEESECAKE, TOAST, OR LASAGNA

SWEET AND SPICY PROSCIUTTO-RICOTTA TOASTS

NOTES / INGREDIENTS / METHOD:

This dish is more of an idea than a recipe. Ricotta and bread are both great blank canvases that you can "paint" with whatever toppings you might have on hand. The balances between sweet and spice, creamy and crunchy, hot and cold, in these toasts make them really fun. People can chop off however much they'd like to eat, adding an interactive element, too.

SLICE THE BREAD
LENGTHWISE

1 baguette
Extra-virgin olive oil
1 shallot, sliced into rings
Kosher salt
2 tablespoons sherry vinegar
1 teaspoon sugar
6 fresh figs

1 pint Homemade Fresh Ricotta (page 57)
4 ounces prosciutto
8 Calabrian or other medium-hot chiles, thinly sliced
3 marjoram sprigs
Freshly ground black pepper

Preheat the oven to 425°F. Slice the baguette in half lengthwise. Trim the bottom edges so the bread will sit flat when facing up. Drizzle some olive oil over the bread and toast in the oven until just golden brown.

Heat a small sauté pan with a coating of olive oil over high heat, then sear the shallot rings until they brown. Sprinkle with salt, add the vinegar and the sugar, followed by a tablespoon of water, then take the pan off the heat.

Slice the figs into circles.

Smear the fresh ricotta onto the toasted bread. Top with the sliced figs, pieces of prosciutto, chiles, and shallot rings. Remove the marjoram leaves from the sprigs and place on top. Drizzle with some more olive oil and season with salt and black pepper. Cut and serve.

← BROWN THE SHALLOTS

ICEBOX STRAWBERRY-RICOTTA CHEESECAKE BOMBE

NOTES / INGREDIENTS / METHOD:

The pain in making cheesecake often lies in the baking step—the fear of the cheesecake drying out or cracking. To solve this, we created a no-bake cheesecake. That's right: you don't have to turn on the oven even once for this dessert. We used whey to dissolve the gelatin that sets the cheese, so we are not diluting the flavor of the homemade ricotta with water. And in order to get a nice snap in the crust, we caramelized the sugar and mixed it with butter and graham crackers to create a pressable crust that doesn't need baking, either. Pressing it into the cold cheese and refrigerating the whole thing sets the crust and, in turn, the refrigerated cheesecake instantly sets the strawberry sauce.

CHEESECAKE
1 cup whey from drained
    Homemade Fresh Ricotta
    (page 57), or water
1 packet unflavored gelatin
1½ cups sugar
1 cup cream cheese, at room
    temperature
3 cups Homemade Fresh Ricotta
    (page 57)
Zest and juice of 1 lemon
½ teaspoon vanilla extract
1 packet of graham crackers
¼ teaspoon ground cinnamon

½ teaspoon salt
½ cup (1 stick) unsalted butter,
    cut into chunks

STRAWBERRY SAUCE
2 packets unflavored gelatin
2 (16-ounce) containers fresh
    strawberries
½ cup sugar
½ teaspoon salt
Juice of ½ lemon

6 small basil leaves

Make the cheesecake Heat the whey just until it comes to a low simmer. Combine the gelatin and ½ cup of the sugar in a bowl. Pour the whey into the gelatin, and whisk to dissolve.

Soften the cream cheese by beating in a stand mixer or with a wooden spoon by hand. Beat in the ricotta. (Adding half, beating, then adding the next half makes it easier to incorporate.)

Pour half the whey-gelatin mixture into the ricotta and mix well. Add the rest of the whey-gelatin mixture and mix to incorporate until smooth. Add the lemon zest, juice, and vanilla.

RECIPE CONTINUES

ADD THE WHEY-GELATIN MIXTURE TO THE RICOTTA

TRANSFER
THE BATTER TO
A PLASTIC - LINED
BOWL

TOP WITH THE
CRUMB MIXTURE

Spray the inside of a large bowl with nonstick spray, and then line it with a large piece of plastic wrap that hangs over the sides (the spray helps the wrap stick). Scoop the cheesecake mixture into the bowl. Tap the bowl against the counter to settle the cheesecake and remove any air bubbles. Cover with the hanging plastic wrap and place in the refrigerator.

Crush the graham crackers into crumbs using a food processor. Transfer into a medium bowl, and mix with the cinnamon and salt.

Add the remaining 1 cup sugar and ½ cup water to a small saucepan over medium heat with a candy thermometer. Cook the syrup until it's a light tannish brown (to 330°F). Take off of the heat and stir in the butter.

Pour the caramel mixture into the graham crumbs and stir together. The caramel will hold the crust together and give it a crackling texture.

Remove the cheesecake from the refrigerator, remove the top layer of plastic wrap, and sprinkle the crumb mixture over the top of the cake. Pat the crumbs down gently using your hands to create a smooth layer. Cover with the plastic wrap again and place back in the refrigerator for at least 3 hours.

Make the strawberry sauce Dissolve the gelatin in ½ cup water in a small bowl, and gently stir to combine.

Reserve 1 cup of smaller strawberries. Remove the stems and hulls from the rest, and slice them in half. Combine with the gelatin mixture, sugar, salt, and lemon juice in a medium saucepan set over medium heat. Simmer until the strawberries are very soft, 10 to 15 minutes. Set a fine strainer over a bowl and strain the strawberry mixture. Very gently press down on the strawberries to release the remaining juices. Allow the mixture to cool to room temperature.

Slice the remaining strawberries in half.

Finish the cake Remove the cheesecake from the refrigerator. Peel the plastic wrap away from the top of the cheesecake, and place a circular piece of cardboard the same size as the cake on top of the bowl. (A flat plate can work too, but it should really be the same size as the cake, so no sauce pools around the bottom.) Holding the bowl and cardboard firmly, flip the bowl over and set onto a rack set over a large plate. Gently remove the bowl and peel off the plastic wrap from the cake. Ladle the strawberry sauce over the cheesecake and allow the excess to drain through the rack. Gently press the halved strawberries into the cheesecake, and top with the basil leaves.

← LADLE SAUCE OVER
THE CHEESECAKE

CHICKEN & TURKEY

Making fried chicken can seem daunting, but after frying thousands of chickens at Wayfare Tavern, we've learned a thing or two. We've developed a recipe for fried chicken that works beautifully in the home; it eliminates the fear of under- or overcooking by roasting the chicken low and slow at first, keeping the meat juicy and flavorful. Then you dip the chicken in batter and fry it quickly for some fantastic, dependable results.

We also wanted to turn a traditional roast chicken into something really memorable, something you'll truly crave, so we found a few tricks to make the skin super-crisp. We've even elevated the leftovers by developing a few new favorite ways to use cold chicken. In fact, the possibilities for serving this leftover roast chicken seem endless (but we won't judge you if you end up eating the leftovers cold, straight from the fridge).

And speaking of leftovers, we started thinking about families gathering for Thanksgiving, generation after generation. We all have our favorite traditions, whether it's making pie with Grandma or playing football in the yard before the feast. Because this is such an important time, I wanted to find a few ways to make Thanksgiving dinner easier to get on the table, and a little more exciting, too. Our Super-Fast Roast Turkey (page 78) takes advantage of a technique called spatchcocking—splitting the bird open to increase the amount of heat that can penetrate the turkey and decrease the cooking time. It guarantees moist, flavorful turkey in way less time. We've also come up with a few spins on Thanksgiving classics, from green beans to gravy to sweet potatoes. I know you and your family will love these recipes on Thanksgiving and year-round.

RECIPES:

- WAYFARE TAVERN'S FRIED CHICKEN 65
- SUPER-CRISP ROAST CHICKEN 69
- THAI CHICKEN SALAD 70
- SEARED AND CHOPPED CHICKEN LIVER TOAST 72
- KALE WALDORF CHICKEN SALAD 75
- BUTTERMILK-HERB DRESSING 76
- SUPER-FAST ROAST TURKEY 78
- THANKSGIVING SAUCE 80
- VEGETARIAN THANKSGIVING SAUCE 81
- UPDATED CRANBERRY SAUCE WITH CELERY-WALNUT SALAD 82
- CRANBERRY "SALAMI" 85
- GREEN BEAN POUTINE 86
- ROASTED SWEET POTATOES WITH ROASTED BANANA SOUR CREAM 88
- TEST KITCHEN STUFFING 90

WAYFARE TAVERN'S FRIED CHICKEN

NOTES / INGREDIENTS / METHOD:

The fried chicken at Wayfare Tavern is always one of our most popular menu items. We sous-vide the chicken pieces in advance, cooking them through in an immersion circulator at a constant low temperature, and then fry them to order, ensuring each guest gets a perfectly cooked piece of chicken. We wanted to create a version, though, for the home kitchen without a sous-vide setup. So, we tested a few versions, and landed on a recipe that involves low-and-slow roasting an herb-rubbed chicken, then finishing the chicken with a quick trip in the fryer after a buttermilk soak. The salt in the herb rub acts as a dry "brine" while the chicken is low roasting.

Each step in this cooking process contributes to the best home-fried chicken we've ever had. The herbs bring the same fresh flavors as we use at Wayfare Tavern, where we serve the plated dish with fresh lemon wedges. This would be a great pairing with the Loaded Iceberg Wedge Salad (page 226).

2 (3- to 3½-pound) organic chickens

FOR THE ROASTING
2 bunches of fresh rosemary
2 bunches of fresh thyme
2 bunches of fresh sage
10 fresh bay leaves
3 garlic cloves
¼ cup olive oil
6 tablespoons freshly ground black pepper
3 tablespoons kosher salt

FOR THE FRYING
1 quart buttermilk
1 tablespoon hot sauce (we like Crystal)
1 teaspoon sugar
1 gallon grapeseed or canola oil
1 head of garlic
4 cups all-purpose flour
1 cup rice flour
½ cup garlic powder
½ cup onion powder
⅓ cup kosher salt
¼ cup freshly ground black pepper
Flaky sea salt
4 lemons, cut into wedges

RECIPE CONTINUES

ROASTING THE CHICKEN LOW AND SLOW MIMICS SOUS-VIDE COOKING

For the roasting Preheat the oven to 200°F. Strip the herbs from the tough stems. Roughly chop one-third each of the rosemary, thyme, and sage, along with half of the bay leaves and the garlic (set remaining herbs and bay leaves aside for frying the chicken). Mix with the olive oil, and add 2 tablespoons pepper and 3 tablespoons salt. Rub the mixture on the birds so the herbs stick to the skin. Place the seasoned birds in a roasting pan and put in the oven.

After 2½ hours, remove the chicken from the oven. The internal temperature between the breast and the thigh near the bone should be 150°F. At this stage, the chicken is cooked three-quarters of the way through. Let cool enough so you can handle the chickens.

For the frying Break the birds into 10 pieces: cut off the wings, the legs, and the thighs, and cut the breast pieces in half. (Save the backs and carcasses for stock or another use.) In a large bowl, season the buttermilk with the hot sauce and sugar. Submerge the chicken in the buttermilk and let sit for 30 minutes.

Add the grapeseed oil to a large, heavy-bottomed pot, making sure there is at least 3 inches of clearance over the level of the oil. Break apart the head of garlic into cloves. Turn the heat on medium-high, and add the remaining rosemary, thyme, sage, and bay leaves, and the garlic cloves to the oil. As the oil heats to 375°F, the herbs and garlic will perfume the oil. (The crisped herbs will also serve as a garnish for the finished dish.) When crisp, transfer the herbs to a paper towel–lined plate. Remove the garlic as well, and reserve for a garnish.

While the oil continues to heat to 375°F, combine the flours, garlic powder, onion powder, ⅓ cup salt, and ¼ cup black pepper in a large bowl and mix thoroughly. Remove the chicken from the buttermilk (do not dry) and coat the chicken well in the flour mixture.

INFUSING OIL WITH HERBS AND
GARLIC IS ONE OF MY FAVORITE TRICKS

With the oil now at 375°F, and without overcrowding the pot, fry the breaded chicken in batches for 6 to 8 minutes, until all of the pieces are golden brown. Remove the chicken to a clean kitchen cloth and season the freshly fried chicken with flaky sea salt and freshly ground pepper.

Use a paper bag, brown parchment paper, or a clean napkin to line the bottom of a serving platter. Pile on the chicken and serve with the crispy herbs, fried garlic, and fresh lemon wedges.

CRISPING CHICKEN THE CHINESE WAY

Getting the perfect roast chicken took us some time, but once we thought through the science involved, we were onto something great. I have always loved the super-crispy texture of Chinese-style pork belly and Peking duck, so we used them as inspiration. The Chinese methods for those dishes call for combining baking soda, sugar, vinegar, and boiling water, and pouring the mixture over the scored skin of pork belly. If it works on pork belly, why wouldn't it work for chicken? The baking soda breaks down the connective tissue between the layers of skin, which both allows it to crisp beautifully and prevents it from getting soggy when it cools down. The sugar caramelizes on the skin, contributing both color and flavor. We also discovered that cooking the chicken on a rack allows air to circulate better around the bird. These elements combined to produce an unbelievably crispy chicken skin encasing juicy meat.

SUPER-CRISP ROAST CHICKEN

NOTES / INGREDIENTS / METHOD:

The perfect roasted chicken is a crowd-pleaser, but a lot of cooks worry about getting the skin crisp while also keeping the meat moist. We tested a variety of methods to see what worked and why: we poached a chicken for 30 minutes before broiling, we roasted one low and slow, we dipped one in a water bath before roasting, we trussed, we didn't truss, we stuffed, we didn't stuff . . . we even cooked one upside down. In the end, we combined a few of the techniques that worked best and drew some inspiration from Asia. We riffed on a Chinese technique to get an unbelievably crispy skin; that is, we poured a baking soda–vinegar solution over the chicken to tighten the skin first. This keeps the skin crisp for hours after roasting.

3 tablespoons white vinegar
2 tablespoons sugar
1½ tablespoons baking soda
1 (4-pound) organic chicken
Kosher salt
Freshly ground black pepper

1½ lemons, cut in half
3 rosemary sprigs
4 bay leaves
3 oregano sprigs
3 thyme sprigs
5 garlic cloves, crushed

Preheat the oven to 400°F. Boil 5 cups of water in a pot over high heat and add the vinegar and sugar. Once the water is boiling, add the baking soda.

Set the chicken on a rack and place it in the sink. Carefully pour the boiling liquid all over the chicken; this sets up the skin to crisp up in the oven. (Pouring the mixture from a teakettle helps to protect you from the steam, but be sure to wash out the kettle afterwards!)

Pat the chicken dry. Liberally season the inside of the chicken with salt and pepper. Squeeze the juice from the lemon halves into the cavity and then add the lemons. Lightly crush the rosemary, bay leaves, oregano, and thyme in your hands and stuff into the cavity along with the garlic cloves.

Season the outside with more salt and pepper, place the bird on a rack, and place both on a sheet pan in the oven. Roast for around 50 minutes, or until the skin is crisp and a thermometer at the joint reads 155°F.

Remove the bird, let it rest for 15 minutes, then carve and serve.

THIS EXTRA STEP MAKES A HUGE DIFFERENCE IN THE FINAL PRODUCT

THAI CHICKEN SALAD

NOTES / INGREDIENTS / METHOD:

The banana in this Thai chicken salad is an unexpected twist, but it adds a unique touch. The dish is a perfect way to use any leftover roasted chicken, but if you have leftovers from our Super-Crisp Roast Chicken (page 69), be sure to save some of the skin to fry up and use as a topping for the salad.

USE LEFTOVER CHICKEN IN THIS
SALAD FOR LUNCH THE NEXT DAY

DRESSING
1 cup mayonnaise
1 cup sour cream
¼ cup coconut milk
3 tablespoons fish sauce
3 tablespoons lime juice
**2 tablespoons light brown
  sugar**

SALAD
1 carrot, peeled
2 green onions
⅓ cucumber
1 serrano chile
**⅓ cup dry-roasted salted
  peanuts**
4 mint sprigs
¼ bunch of cilantro

1 ripe banana
**½ leftover roasted chicken,
  including skin if possible**
Kosher salt
Freshly ground black pepper
1 lime

TOPPING
⅓ cup bean sprouts
1 tablespoon rice vinegar
1 teaspoon fish sauce
Kosher salt
Freshly ground black pepper

**6 to 8 leaves butter lettuce
  or red romaine, about
  2 or 3 leaves per person**
Lime wedges

Make the dressing Whisk together the mayonnaise, sour cream, and coconut milk. Add the fish sauce, lime juice, and brown sugar, and whisk again.

Make the salad Slice the carrot into thin planks lengthwise, and then cut into matchsticks. Thinly slice the green portion of the green onions. Slice the cucumber and chile into thin rounds. Chop the peanuts. Pick the mint and cilantro leaves off the stems and add the leaves. Smash the banana with a fork in a large mixing bowl.

If you have leftover chicken skin, briefly shallow-fry the skin in some oil or reroast in a 350°F oven to crisp it. Pull the chicken meat into shreds into the bowl with the banana. Drizzle half of the dressing into the bowl and mix with the chicken. Season with salt and freshly ground black pepper. Squeeze in lime juice to taste, for brightness.

Make the topping In a separate bowl, combine the bean sprouts, cilantro and mint leaves, carrot matchsticks, green onion slices, cucumber, chile, and peanuts. Add the rice vinegar and fish sauce, and toss. Season with salt and pepper, if needed.

Place the chicken salad in a large serving dish. Top with the bean sprout mixture and crunch the fried chicken skin on top, if using. Serve with the lettuce leaves, lime wedges, and the rest of the dressing on the side. If desired, guests scoop the salad into lettuce cups to eat.

IT MIGHT SEEM CRAZY, BUT YOU'LL LOVE THE BANANA

025 SEARED AND CHOPPED CHICKEN LIVER TOAST

4

NOTES / INGREDIENTS / METHOD:

A lot of times, people throw away the chicken livers that come with a roasting chicken, but in my restaurants we send them out to VIPs or the staff eats them because they are so delicious. Most chopped chicken liver recipes have you puree the livers, which can be delicious, but we wanted to chop them instead, for a more interesting textural experience. Madeira wine and chicken liver are an ideal combination: the iron-rich livers are balanced by the sweet and acidic Madeira.

EASIEST GARLIC
BREAD: RUB
THE CLOVES
ON TOAST

2 shallots
4 tablespoons (½ stick) unsalted butter
Extra-virgin olive oil
Kosher salt
1 cup Madeira (or ruby port or brandy)

1 pound chicken livers
1 bunch of parsley, stems removed
Freshly ground black pepper
4 thick slices of sourdough bread
1 garlic clove
Flaky sea salt

REALLY BROWN THE SHALLOTS BEFORE ADDING THE MADEIRA

Slice the shallots into small rings. Melt 2 tablespoons of the butter with 2 tablespoons of the olive oil in a large sauté pan over medium heat, then add the shallots. Cook until the shallots are deep brown, then season with salt and deglaze the pan with the Madeira. Reduce the wine to a glaze, and pour the shallot mixture into a bowl. Wipe out the pan with a paper towel.

Trim off the sinewy sections of the livers. Pat the livers dry; if they're too moist, they will steam instead of caramelize. Add 2 tablespoons of olive oil to the pan, and heat over medium-high until the oil is shimmering. Season the livers with salt, and place them in the pan with space around each liver. Don't move them until they turn golden brown on the bottom. Flip, adding the remaining 2 tablespoons butter. This will deglaze the pan and start to build a sauce. Add the shallot mixture back to the pan and cook together for a few seconds.

Transfer the livers and sauce to a cutting board. Place the parsley leaves on top of the livers, and chop the parsley and chicken livers together. Season with salt and freshly ground pepper to taste.

Brush the bread slices with some olive oil, and grill on a grill pan or in the broiler until toasted on both sides. Remove from the pan and rub the pieces with the garlic. The toasted edges will slightly break down the garlic so the toast takes on the garlic flavor. Top the toast with the chicken liver and parsley mixture, and finish with a brushing of olive oil and a sprinkling of flaky sea salt.

KALE WALDORF CHICKEN SALAD

NOTES / INGREDIENTS / METHOD:

This is also a great use for any leftover roasted chicken (see page 69). We elevated the classic Waldorf salad by using a chiffonade of kale and by roasting the grapes to concentrate their flavor. This salad also has a great all-around dressing for other salads or for dipping.

Extra-virgin olive oil
2 cups seedless red grapes, on the stem
1 bunch of lacinato kale (also called Tuscan kale, dinosaur kale, or cavolo nero)
½ leftover roasted chicken
1 Honeycrisp apple
½ cup sliced celery

½ cup celery leaves
⅓ cup chopped walnuts
⅓ cup crumbled blue cheese
Buttermilk-Herb Dressing (page 76), as needed
Juice of 1 lemon
Kosher salt
Freshly ground black pepper

Preheat the oven to 350°F.

Heat a large, oven-safe sauté pan over medium-high heat with 3 tablespoons olive oil and add the grape clusters. Toss lightly in the oil, then move to the oven and roast for 10 minutes, until the grapes shrivel or burst. When cooled, remove the grapes from the stems.

Thinly chop the kale. Pull the chicken meat into bite-size shreds. Cut the apple into matchsticks.

Pile the chicken, grapes, and kale onto a large cutting board, and add the celery and its leaves, walnuts, and cheese. Chop all the ingredients together until you have bite-size pieces.

Serve on the cutting board or put the salad into a large bowl. Drizzle the desired amount of dressing over the top. Pour the lemon juice over the salad, and drizzle with more olive oil. Season with salt and pepper, toss, and serve.

ROASTING GRAPES CONCENTRATES THEIR FLAVOR

BUTTERMILK-HERB DRESSING

Makes 1 pint

½ cup mayonnaise

½ cup sour cream

¾ cup buttermilk

2 tablespoons chopped fresh dill

3 tablespoons chopped parsley

2 tablespoons chopped chives

1½ teaspoons chopped fresh tarragon

Juice of ½ lemon

½ teaspoon salt, or more to taste

½ teaspoon black pepper, or more to taste

Add all of the ingredients to a medium bowl and whisk to combine. Season to taste with more salt and pepper. The dressing keeps in the refrigerator for 5 days.

THIS VERSATILE DRESSING IS DELICIOUS AS A DIP

THE TROUBLE WITH TURKEY

Every year, the Butterball Turkey Hotline helps thousands get Thanksgiving dinner on the table. By calming nerves and guiding home cooks through the process, they make Thanksgiving happen for tons of families. But there is always a lot of anxiety around turkey. Often, Thanksgiving is the only meal that home cooks make for their whole families, and they want it to be perfect. They want to present their families with a Norman Rockwell–worthy bird. That's a pretty big task for people who don't roast birds on a regular basis.

We wanted to take the anxiety out of Thanksgiving and create a foolproof way to cook that turkey. We first made the Butterball recipe. But right off the bat, the instructions are a bit confusing. The Butterball recipe indicates that for a bird that is between 9 and 18 pounds, the cooking time is from 3¾ to 4½ hours. Those are very wide ranges! You might overcook (or undercook) your turkey if you are going purely on time. And that's exactly what happened to us when we followed those directions: when we pulled out our bird at the 3-hour mark, it was already overcooked.

Wanting to take some of the guesswork out of the cooking time, we thought about butterflying, or spatchcocking, the turkey. Think of it this way: Turkeys vary tremendously in size, but if you split it open and flatten it out, the size difference matters a lot less in the oven because you don't have a big, cold center fighting against the heat.

Prepared this way, our turkey cooked in 1 hour and 45 minutes, saving 1 hour and 15 minutes, and our bird was beautifully juicy.

SUPER-FAST ROAST TURKEY

NOTES / INGREDIENTS / METHOD:

The Thanksgiving turkey is the centerpiece of the meal, but, despite its being cooked every year for generations, it still causes anxiety. The annual conundrum? Getting a flavorful turkey that also looks good—and the rest of dinner—on the table before the grandparents fall asleep.

The first thing we realized was that stuffing the turkey only makes things harder: if you stuff your turkey, you create a very dense material for heat to travel through, and by the time the stuffing is hot in the center, the breast meat of the turkey is totally overcooked. Instead, we piped the stuffing between the skin and the breast. That way, you still get flavorful stuffing while protecting the breast.

We also spatchcocked the turkey. Before you turn and run, let me tell you that it shaved off an hour and 15 minutes of cooking time from the standard Butterball turkey instructions. Spatchcocking simply means removing the backbone, increasing the bird's surface area, and letting the oven's heat into the cavity much faster. This allows the turkey to cook in way less time than traditional recipes and keeps it juicy. You'll notice that we didn't brine the bird: we found that spatchcocking gave us a juicy and tender bird without brining, which was great, since most people don't have refrigerator space for an entire turkey in a brine bucket.

You can have your butcher spatchcock the turkey if you'd like; just ask for the backbone if you make our Thanksgiving Sauce (page 80).

One (10-pound) turkey
1 recipe **Test Kitchen Stuffing** (page 90), in a piping bag or zip-top plastic bag with a corner snipped off

Grapeseed or vegetable oil, as needed
Kosher salt
Freshly ground black pepper
1 bunch of sage
1 bunch of thyme

Preheat the oven to 375°F.

Remove the heart and giblets and reserve; discard the liver. Flip the turkey upside down so the breast is on your cutting board. Using kitchen shears, cut on both sides of the backbone so the bone can be removed. Pull the bone out of the turkey and reserve. Gently but firmly open up the bird a little (you can flatten it if you'd like) and set it on your board with the skin side up.

REMOVE THE BACKBONE WITH KITCHEN SHEARS

GENTLY LOOSEN THE SKIN FROM THE BREAST

Insert your fingers gently between the skin and breast meat, separating the two while keeping the skin attached. You want to create a pocket for the stuffing without tearing the skin.

Pipe the stuffing underneath the skin of the bird, creating a layer between the meat and the skin. Rub grapeseed oil over the skin, and season liberally with salt and pepper. Do the same to the underside of the bird.

THIS TURKEY COOKS IN WAY LESS TIME

Place a large rack on a roasting pan or sheet pan, and put the whole sprigs of herbs on top of the rack. Put the turkey skin side up on top of the herbs. Sandwiching the herbs between the rack and the turkey will prevent them from burning. Put the turkey in the oven and cook for 1 hour and 15 minutes. At this point, the skin should be golden brown and the temperature should be 135°F. To take the temperature, insert a meat thermometer into the thickest part of the thigh, staying away from hitting the bone. Tent the turkey with tin foil and continue to roast until the temperature reaches 160°F in the leg, about another 30 minutes. (The internal temperature will continue to rise as it rests.)

Remove the turkey and let it rest for 15 minutes before slicing.

029–030 THANKSGIVING SAUCE

BROWN THOROUGHLY FOR YOUR FLAVOR BASE

GET ALL THE FOND !

NOTES / INGREDIENTS / METHOD:

Why is it that every photo of Thanksgiving dinner shows the gravy on the turkey, when everyone really loves to put the gravy all over their plate? We set out to make a gravy that is lightened up, that doesn't rely on heavy roux or cornstarch for thickening, but is flavorful and goes with every part of the dinner. Our key was to use pureed vegetables for flavor and body, and that inspired us to make a meat-free version, too, so that vegetarians could also enjoy pure Thanksgiving in a bite.

1 turkey backbone
  (from spatchcocked turkey,
  see page 78)
1 turkey neck bone
¼ cup grapeseed or vegetable oil
¼ pound bacon, cut into lardons
2 cups diced onions
1 cup diced carrots
1 cup diced celery

1 cup diced butternut squash
1 garlic clove, chopped
Kosher salt
Reserved heart and giblets from
  the turkey (do not use the liver)
5 thyme sprigs
4 sage sprigs
Freshly ground black pepper

Cut the turkey backbone and neck bone into 2-inch pieces.

Heat a stockpot over medium-high heat and add the oil. When the oil is shimmering, add the bones and brown, turning as the sides become a deep caramel, about 10 minutes. Remove the turkey bones from the pot and set them aside, then add the bacon lardons to the pot and turn the heat down to medium. Cook the bacon until it is rendered and crisp. Add the onions, carrots, celery, squash, and garlic to the bacon and caramelize the vegetables, about 10 minutes.

Continuously scrape the bottom of the pan with a wooden spoon to incorporate the brown fond. Once the vegetables caramelize, add a few pinches of salt. Add the turkey bones back to the pot with the heart, giblets, thyme, and sage, followed by 4 cups of water. Bring to a simmer, then turn to low and cook for 45 minutes, until the vegetables are very soft, then turn off the heat.

Remove the bones, giblets, heart, and tough herb stems and discard. Transfer the liquid, vegetables, and bacon to a blender and puree until smooth. If necessary, thin the sauce with hot water until you reach the consistency of gravy. Add salt and pepper to taste, and serve.

VEGETARIAN THANKSGIVING SAUCE

Makes 1½ quarts

¼ cup grapeseed or vegetable oil
2 cups diced onions
1 cup diced carrots
1 cup diced celery
1 cup butternut squash
1 garlic clove, chopped
Kosher salt

Two 2-by-6-inch strips dried
  kombu
1 ounce dried shiitake mushrooms
5 thyme sprigs
4 sage sprigs
Freshly ground black pepper
½ teaspoon lemon juice

Heat the oil in a stockpot over medium-high heat. When the oil shimmers, add the onions, carrots, celery, squash, and garlic, and cook, stirring, until the vegetables caramelize, about 10 minutes. Continuously scrape the bottom of the pan with a wooden spoon to incorporate the brown fond. Once they have browned, add a few generous pinches of salt and 4 cups of water, followed by the kombu, mushrooms, thyme, and sage. Bring the mixture up to a simmer, then turn the heat down to low and cook for 45 minutes, then turn off the heat.

Pull out the kombu strips and tough herb stems and discard. Transfer the vegetables and liquid to a blender. Holding the top, blend the vegetables until completely smooth. Thin out with hot water if necessary to reach a gravy consistency and season with salt and pepper to taste. Add the lemon juice. Serve.

MUSHROOMS AND KOMBU GIVE MEATY DEPTH

UPDATED CRANBERRY SAUCE WITH CELERY-WALNUT SALAD

COOK THE CRANBERRIES UNTIL JAMMY

REFRIGERATE UNTIL SET

NOTES / INGREDIENTS / METHOD:

When I was growing up, our family's Thanksgiving table was always graced by cranberry sauce that my mother seemingly slaved away over all night. It was this gorgeous cylinder with all these beautiful ridges that looked like the inside of a can. We'd ooh and aah, but the craziest thing was, we never saw her make the sauce!

So we set out to create a more delicious, homemade version of that classic, making an orange-infused sauce and letting it set overnight in a loaf pan, then topped it off with a crunchy celery-walnut salad.

36 ounces fresh or frozen whole cranberries, ¼ cup set aside
2 cups diced pineapple
1 tablespoon orange zest
3 cups sugar
1 tablespoon lemon juice

2 celery ribs, including leaves
¼ bunch chives
2 tablespoons walnuts
Olive oil
Kosher salt
Freshly ground black pepper

Place the cranberries (keep the extra ¼ cup in the refrigerator), pineapple, orange zest, sugar, lemon juice, and ½ cup of water in a large saucepan. Bring to a simmer over medium heat, then reduce to a very low simmer and allow to reduce slowly, 30 to 40 minutes. Stir often so it does not burn. It will look like warmed jam once it is done.

Spray the inside of a loaf pan or other rectangular dish with nonstick spray. (A 1½-quart dish makes for a nice shape.) Line the pan with plastic wrap, and press so the plastic tightly adheres to the pan. Pour the sauce into the pan. Tap the pan against the counter a few times to release any air bubbles. Fold the plastic wrap back over the loaf pan, and refrigerate for at least 3 hours, or overnight, until set.

The next morning, gently invert the cranberry loaf onto a plate and remove the plastic wrap.

Using a vegetable peeler, create long curls of celery and immerse in ice water so they stay curly. Finely mince the chives. Remove the celery curls from the ice water, drain, and toss with the chives. Top the cranberry loaf with the curls and chives, then add the celery leaves. Rough chop the walnuts and add to the loaf as well. Top with the reserved ¼ cup cranberries. Drizzle with olive oil, and season with salt and pepper. Serve.

SERVE THE "SALAMI" WITH
A MILD CHEESE

CRANBERRY "SALAMI"

NOTES / INGREDIENTS / METHOD:

After we made our Updated Cranberry Sauce (page 82), we got to thinking about how that sauce holds its shape because cranberries have a ton of natural pectin—they turn into a natural jelly on their own. So we played around with that idea and came up with forming it into a sliceable salami shape, which makes a delicious cheese accompaniment to start off the feast. See the Fig-Hazelnut Fruit "Salami" (page 54) for a similar idea.

4 cups sugar
½ cup chopped walnuts
36 ounces fresh or frozen cranberries, ¼ cup set aside

2 cups diced pineapple
1 tablespoon orange zest
1 tablespoon lemon juice

Add 1 cup of the sugar to a small saucepan with 1 cup of water and bring it to a boil. Add the walnuts, lower the heat, and stir. Poach the walnuts until they are softened, about 10 minute, then strain them.

Place the cranberries (keep the extra ¼ cup in the refrigerator), pineapple, orange zest, the remaining 3 cups sugar, lemon juice, and ½ cup of water in a large saucepan. Bring to a simmer over medium heat, then reduce to a very low simmer and allow to reduce slowly, 30 to 40 minutes. Stir often so it does not burn. It will look very thick, like jam, once it is done. Fold in the reserved cranberries and walnuts and let cool for 10 minutes, until cool enough to handle.

Lay a sheet of plastic wrap, about 28 inches long, on a flat surface. Form the cranberry mixture into a log along the length of the plastic wrap, 1 inch from the bottom of the plastic. The log should be about 2 inches in diameter and 18 inches long. Smooth the log with a spatula, fold the plastic wrap over the log, and gently roll into a smooth cylinder. Continue rolling up the cranberry until you get to the end of the plastic wrap. Pinch the edges of the plastic to tighten the cylinder, and twist the ends in opposite directions to tighten further. Roll another layer of plastic around the log, wrapping around the twisted ends so they don't unravel. Refrigerate the log overnight so that it sets. If desired, gently remove the plastic wrap from the log after it's set and wrap tightly with layers of cheesecloth to have more of a cured-salami kind of look. Keep refrigerated until ready to serve.

GREEN BEAN POUTINE

8

NOTES / INGREDIENTS / METHOD:

We wanted to deconstruct the classic green bean casserole that graces Thanksgiving tables around the country. Instead of overcooked green beans and canned soup, we wanted to highlight the quality of the vegetables, but we also wanted to have a little fun. So we took inspiration from poutine—a pile of French fries, gravy, and cheese—and we combined green beans with a great mushroom gravy and fresh burrata cheese to make our Thanksgiving version of it. Who would complain about that?

ADD THE MUSHROOMS

¼ cup grapeseed or vegetable oil
1 bunch sage leaves, with the stems
½ medium onion, diced
2 garlic cloves, finely chopped
Kosher salt
½ pound brown button mushrooms
3 to 4 ounces maitake mushrooms
3 to 4 ounces brown beech mushrooms

½ cup sherry
1½ cups heavy cream
Freshly ground black pepper
1½ pounds green beans
1 bunch chives
1 package burrata, about 4 ounces
½ cup fried onions, such as Durkee's or French's
Extra-virgin olive oil, to finish

Heat the oil in a large saucepan over medium heat, and when the oil looks wavy, fry the sage leaves. This both infuses the oil and provides a garnish for the final dish.

Remove the sage once it is crisp and drain on paper towels. Add the onion and garlic to the oil with ¼ teaspoon salt to sweat them down, stirring occasionally so they don't brown unevenly.

While the onion is cooking, wipe the mushrooms clean, then quarter them and add them to the saucepan. Cook the mushrooms until they have released their liquid and it has evaporated and they get a bit of caramelization on the edges. Add the sherry to deglaze the pan. Then add the cream and salt to taste. Simmer to reduce the cream and sherry by about half, approximately 10 minutes. It should be nice and thick. Season with freshly ground black pepper and more salt, if necessary. Keep warm over very low heat at the back of the stove.

Preheat the oven to broil.

MUSHROOMS + CREAM = DELICIOUS

Heat a large pot of water to boil and generously salt the water so it is as salty as the sea. Blanch the green beans until cooked but still crunchy, 1½ to 2 minutes. Drain the green beans and spread them out on a sheet pan, so they cool down quickly. (We recommend not shocking them in ice water, because the flavor will wash off.)

Finely mince the chives and add them to the mushroom sauce.

Transfer the green beans to a cast-iron pan or other oven-safe dish. Spoon the mushroom sauce over the beans.

Tear the burrata into chunks and top the green beans. Place the green beans in the broiler so the cheese gets melty. Remove from the oven and top with some of the reserved sage leaves—we used 3. Sprinkle the fried onions over the top, as desired, and drizzle with olive oil.

SPOON SAUCE OVER THE BEANS

ROASTED SWEET POTATOES WITH ROASTED BANANA SOUR CREAM

NOTES / INGREDIENTS / METHOD:

I love the combination of roasted sweet potatoes and bananas. I've made a whipped sweet potato and roasted banana dish many times, but this being the Test Kitchen, we wanted to reinvent the wheel a little bit. Instead of mashed sweet potatoes, we roasted them in wedges, bringing some texture to the Thanksgiving table. A roasted banana sour cream provides the tanginess, and serrano chiles bring some heat. It's a new twist that your guests will love.

4 medium-size sweet potatoes
2 tablespoons extra-virgin olive oil, plus more for finishing
Sea salt
Freshly ground black pepper
1 banana, unpeeled
4 slices of bacon

1 teaspoon grapeseed or vegetable oil
1 medium onion, sliced into thin rings
1 serrano chile (2 if desired)
1 cup sour cream
¼ bunch chives

ROAST THE SWEET POTATO WEDGES

Preheat the oven to 400°F.

Trim the ends off the sweet potatoes and cut each into 8 wedges. Toss with the 2 tablespoons of olive oil and season generously with salt and pepper. Spread the potatoes on a sheet pan, with the whole banana, and roast in the oven.

Cut the bacon into lardons. Heat the oil in a sauté pan over medium-high heat and cook the bacon until just turning crisp.

Add the onion to the bacon. Thinly slice the serrano chile and add it to the pan along with a pinch of salt. Cook until the onion is caramelized, then turn off the heat.

After the banana is in the oven for 10 to 15 minutes, its skin should be black and it should be very tender. Remove it from the oven, and when cool enough to handle, peel and add the roasted fruit to a blender with the sour cream. Puree until smooth with a few pinches of salt, to taste.

LET THE ONION REALLY CARAMELIZE

After 30 minutes of roasting, the sweet potatoes should be cooked and slightly caramelized at the edges. Transfer to a serving dish. Top with the onions, bacon, and chile. If desired, thinly slice the second serrano chile and add on top. Drizzle with the banana sour cream. Mince the chives and sprinkle on top of the potatoes. Season with sea salt and drizzle with olive oil, then serve.

THESE ARE GREAT YEAR-ROUND

TEST KITCHEN STUFFING

MAKES ENOUGH TO STUFF 1 TURKEY

TOSS BREAD WITH VEGGIES AND SAUSAGE

NOTES / INGREDIENTS / METHOD:

People love the taste of stuffing that's been cooked in the turkey, but usually by the time the stuffing is ready, the bird is overcooked. To combat this problem, and to keep our turkey juicy, we piped the stuffing under the skin instead of filling the cavity. You'll get incredibly flavorful stuffing without overcooked turkey. If you really love stuffing, you can double the recipe and bake half in the oven rather than piping it into the bird.

4 cups of sourdough bread torn into 1-inch pieces, without the crusts

2 tablespoons grapeseed or vegetable oil

½ pound sage breakfast sausage, crumbled

½ cup diced carrots

½ cup diced celery

½ cup diced onion

5 sage leaves

3 thyme sprigs

Kosher salt

Freshly ground black pepper

⅔ cup chicken stock

1 egg

Preheat the oven to 375°F. Toast the bread on a sheet pan in the oven for about 15 minutes, until crisp and golden.

Heat the oil over medium-high heat in a large saucepan, then add the sausage and let it brown. After it's nice and golden on one side, stir to get color all over. Add the carrots, celery, and onion, followed by the sage and thyme, turn the heat down to medium, and cook, stirring occasionally to keep the cooking even. Season with salt and pepper. When the vegetables are aromatic and tender, add a splash of water if necessary to loosen the brown bits from the bottom of the pan. Add the toasted bread and the chicken stock and mix.

Remove the thyme sprigs and pull the leaves off, adding the leaves back to the stuffing, and then transfer the stuffing to a food processor. Process until fairly smooth, adding the egg while pureeing. (If you're doubling the recipe for extra stuffing, puree only half the stuffing; the rest you can bake as directed below.)

Transfer the stuffing to a piping bag (or a large zip-top bag with a corner snipped off).

If you would like to have the stuffing as a stand-alone dish, skip the pureeing. Transfer the stuffing mixture to a greased baking dish and cook in a 350°F oven until the top is golden brown.

PIPE THE STUFFING UNDER THE SKIN

EGGS & SOUFFLÉS

Often, you'll hear that cooking an egg perfectly is the ultimate test of a great chef. At the end of the day, it's about controlling time and temperature, so it's also a skill worth perfecting for the home cook. Still, we wanted to find ways to cook eggs that would give you great results, easily and reliably. (Especially when you're trying to impress someone and want to make it worth his or her while to get out of bed.)

So we developed new, fail-safe ways to conquer breakfast, simple enough to tackle before you've finished your first cup of coffee. We give you new methods for poaching eggs, whether for one or a crowd, as well as tips for making the creamiest scrambled eggs, perfectly rolled omelets, airy soufflés, and perfect boiled eggs.

But aren't boiled eggs the easiest thing in the world to make anyway? Well, I always have deviled eggs on the menus in my restaurants, and the difference between an egg with the yolk set just right and centered and one that's off-kilter with an overcooked yolk is enormous.

When I was growing up in the South, deviled eggs were a constant. My grandmother would make them with a little paprika sprinkled on the creamy yolk, creating that classic we've all had at potlucks and barbecues. They are a delicious taste of nostalgia; and judging from how often people order them, I guess they are for many others, too. Here, I add a few twists that my grandmother didn't teach me but of which I think she would be proud.

RECIPES:

- SUPER-CREAMY SCRAMBLED EGGS 93
- THE EGG-ROLL OMELET 94
- NO-SWEAT POACHED EGGS 96
- ~~THRE~~ THREE-MINUTE BLENDER HOLLANDAISE 97
- CALIFORNIA AVOCADO EGGS BENEDICT 98
- PERFECT STEAMED "BOILED" EGGS 101
- CLASSIC DEVILED EGGS 102
- CAESAR SALAD "DEVILED EGGS" 104
- INFALLIBLE CHOCOLATE SOUFFLÉS 106

SUPER-CREAMY SCRAMBLED EGGS

NOTES / INGREDIENTS / METHOD:

Nine times out of ten, scrambled eggs are overcooked, making them dry and rubbery. It's easy to overcook eggs in a pan over hot direct heat, but when they are cooked in a double boiler with steam as the heat source, the temperature never rises above 212°F (our cooking surface itself didn't rise above 175°F). The double-boiler method produces small, consistently creamy curds of egg. The key is patience and consistent stirring, so all the eggs stay the same temperature throughout.

3 tablespoons unsalted butter
6 large eggs

Kosher salt
Freshly ground black pepper

Fill a saucepan with 2 cups of water and set on the stove. Fit a metal mixing bowl on top, wide enough to cover the pan but not deep enough to touch the water.

Cut 2 tablespoons of the butter into small dice. Crack the eggs into a bowl, season with 2 generous pinches of salt, and beat with a fork until just combined.

Turn the heat to medium under the saucepan. When you see some steam escaping from the pan, add the tablespoon of uncut butter to the bowl. Once the butter is melted, add the eggs and the diced butter, and stir constantly with a rubber spatula, making sure to get around the edges of the bowl. It will take a while, but the curds will come together. The eggs should not get hotter than 165°F; they will be super-creamy as they cook, hovering between liquid and solid. Once the curds come together into a rich custard, the eggs are cooked. Remove them from the bowl immediately and season with salt and pepper.

THE DOUBLE BOILER WILL MAKE THE BEST EGGS YOU'VE HAD

ALL YOU NEED FOR THE PERFECT MORNING

037

THE EGG-ROLL OMELET

CAREFULLY POUR THE EGGS INTO THE LINED SHEET PAN

NOTES / INGREDIENTS / METHOD:

The tricky part of making omelets is usually the flip; one wrong move and you end up with a scramble rather than a neatly folded omelet. But slow-baking and *rolling* an omelet eliminate that flip and also make enough for a whole party at once instead of one omelet at a time. The parchment-paper overhang is the key to making this work; it keeps the eggs in one flat sheet and gives you the ability to roll them up and off the baking sheet once they are done. We added spinach, mushrooms, and brie to our omelet, but you could include any of your favorite toppings. Serve the omelet with a simple salad of herbs, mixed greens, and radishes, if desired.

1 dozen large eggs
½ cup heavy cream
Kosher salt
4 tablespoons (½ stick) unsalted butter, melted
1 bunch of chives
8 ounces brie cheese

1 bunch of baby spinach, cleaned
6 ounces fresh mushrooms, cleaned (chanterelles are really great here)
6 bacon slices, cut into small pieces
1 garlic clove
Freshly ground black pepper

Preheat the oven to 250°F.

Crack the eggs into a large mixing bowl and whisk until slightly frothy. Pour in the cream and season with 1 teaspoon salt. Whisk in the melted butter.

Lightly spray a sheet pan with 1-inch-tall sides with cooking spray, then add a large piece of parchment paper with about a 1-inch overhang on all sides. Smooth out any air bubbles or wrinkles with your hands; it is very important that the parchment is smooth and overhanging on all sides, to ensure the egg mixture does not drift between the pan and the parchment. Spray the paper as well.

Carefully pour the egg mixture onto the sheet pan. It should fill up about halfway. Bake for 25 minutes, or until the eggs are set but still light colored.

GENTLY ROLL THE COOKED EGGS USING THE PAPER AS A HANDLE

While the eggs are cooking, finely mince the chives and cut the brie into small chunks. Lightly chop the spinach and mushrooms.

In a medium sauté pan over medium heat, cook the bacon until crisp. Add the mushrooms and whole garlic. Once the mushrooms are cooked, add the spinach and gently wilt, seasoning with salt and pepper. Turn off the heat. Remove the garlic.

Scatter the top of the eggs with the brie, then the bacon-spinach-mushroom mixture. Place back in the oven for about 3 minutes, until the cheese melts.

Lift up the overhanging portion of one edge of the eggs on the long side of the parchment paper, so the egg sheet on that end folds over on itself. Continue lifting and rolling until you get to the opposite edge of the sheet pan. Then, use both overhanging sides to lift the omelet roll and transfer to a large serving platter, rolling the omelet onto the platter with the seam side down. Serve immediately.

RELEASE THE ROLLED OMELET ONTO A SERVING PLATTER

A SUPER-EASY, ELEGANT BRUNCH FOR A CROWD

038

NO-SWEAT POACHED EGGS

MAKES 12
POACHED EGGS

NOTES / INGREDIENTS / METHOD:

The idea of making eggs Benedict for a crowd can be daunting: poaching one perfect egg in a pot of water is hard enough, but poaching multiple eggs is a test of skill and timing. It turns out that a muffin tin is the answer. Here's our foolproof way to poach multiple eggs at the same time without worrying about them falling apart or having the first batch be cold by the time you're done with the last.

2 teaspoons white vinegar
1 teaspoon salt
12 large eggs

Special equipment: muffin tin with 12 slots, preferably nonstick

OUR SETUP MAKES
12 PERFECT ~~ELLS~~
POACHED EGGS AT
A TIME

Combine 1 cup of water with the vinegar and salt in a 2-cup measure. Fill each muffin cup of the muffin tin with 2 teaspoons of the vinegar mixture. Crack an egg into each slot.

Fill a roasting pan that the muffin tin will easily fit into with 1 inch of water. Place the roasting pan on the stove over medium heat and bring the water to a gentle simmer. Carefully place the muffin tin in the roasting pan and cover the whole thing with foil. Cook the eggs for 5 minutes for a set white and a runny yolk.

Remove the muffin tin from the roasting pan and gently scoop the eggs out of the muffin cups. Serve as desired.

SCOOP OUT THE EGGS AND
SERVE

THREE-MINUTE BLENDER HOLLANDAISE

MAKES ABOUT 1 CUP

NOTES / INGREDIENTS / METHOD:

Lemony, buttery, warm, and rich, hollandaise is one of the most delicious of all sauces, but also one that makes even professional cooks nervous. You'll never have to freak out about it, though—we've found an easy, fast way to bring it to the table. Brunch has never been less stressful. Serve the hollandaise on eggs Benedict (see page 98), if desired.

2 large egg yolks
1 tablespoon fresh lemon juice
Pinch of cayenne

½ cup (1 stick) unsalted butter, melted and kept warm
1 teaspoon kosher salt

Put the egg yolks, lemon juice, cayenne, and 2 tablespoons of warm water in a blender. Pulse a couple of times to combine. Run the blender for 10 seconds, and then, with the blender running, gradually pour the warm melted butter into the egg to make a smooth sauce. If the sauce is very thick, blend in a teaspoon of warm water to loosen it up.

Season the hollandaise with the salt and serve immediately, or keep warm in a small heatproof bowl set over hot (but not simmering) water until ready to serve.

POUR THE MELTED BUTTER INTO THE BLENDER

GENEROUSLY TOP THE EGGS WITH THE SAUCE →

CALIFORNIA AVOCADO EGGS BENEDICT

4

NOTES / INGREDIENTS / METHOD:

Eggs Benedict gets a lot easier with our Three-Minute Blender Hollandaise and No-Sweat Poached Eggs. I like those rich flavors to be balanced with fresh herbs, and creamy avocado is always welcome with eggs, in my opinion. You could add the traditional Canadian bacon if you want, but I love these as they are. This dish is so easy to assemble, and it will be devoured in seconds once it's plated.

4 English muffins, preferably not pre-split

4 tablespoons (½ stick) unsalted butter, melted

8 No-Sweat Poached Eggs (page 96)

1 cup Three-Minute Blender Hollandaise (page 97)

1 Hass avocado, cut into wedges

4 radishes, shaved

1 bunch of chives, minced

½ bunch of upland cress or watercress, leaves only

¼ bunch of tarragon, leaves only

½ pound ricotta salata cheese

Flaky sea salt

Freshly ground black pepper

Extra-virgin olive oil

Preheat the oven to 350°F. Brush the outside tops and bottoms of the English muffins with the melted butter. Place them on a rack on a baking sheet, and toast in the oven for 10 to 15 minutes, or until they are crisp and very hot. Once they have rested for a moment, cut them open.

Place 1 poached egg onto each English muffin half. Spoon 1 to 2 tablespoons of hollandaise over each egg. Serve with wedges of avocado and shaved radishes, and top with the chives, cress, and tarragon. Crumble the ricotta salata over the tops. Season with the flaky sea salt, pepper, and a drizzle of olive oil. Serve immediately.

YOU CAN'T GO WRONG WITH FRESH HERBS AND VEGETABLES

THIS IS GREAT FOR A CROWD

TEST:

THE BOILED EGG TEST

Boiling an egg might sound like the easiest thing in the world, but considering the number of deviled eggs made in my restaurants, we've learned that not all boiled eggs are created equal. You want an egg that is easy to peel, with a golden or pale yolk, for the best texture and flavor, and you want that yolk suspended right in the center of the white for the best presentation.

So we wanted to test some old wives' tales about the best way to boil an egg. One is to add salt to the boiling water, and another is to add baking soda. These both alter the pH of the solution. After our test, though, we found that both methods gave similar results. The eggs were fairly easy to peel, but not any easier than if we had not added the salt or baking soda. We then tried *steaming* the eggs instead of boiling them; these turned out perfectly and, more important, the results were consistent. By steaming the eggs, we exposed them to a constant temperature rather than an environment in which the temperature could vary by as much as 30 degrees, depending on the method used; what's more important, they were much easier to peel and the yolks were centered. And this method works equally well for a range of doneness levels.

PERFECT STEAMED "BOILED" EGGS

MAKES 12
BOILED EGGS

041

NOTES / INGREDIENTS / METHOD:

Steaming is now our favorite method for making "boiled" eggs. First, it's faster because you need to heat up only a small amount of water, rather than bring a full pot to a boil. Second, the heat source remains consistently at 212°F, so the result of timing the cooking is more consistent. And, as a bonus, there is less risk of breakage or cracking, since the eggs aren't bouncing around in roiling, boiling water.

12 eggs (or as many as you want to make)

Fit a colander that can hold all the eggs into a larger pot. Pour 1 inch or more of water under the colander, making sure the level of the water doesn't reach the bottom of the colander. Turn the heat to medium-high. As the water comes to a simmer, add the eggs to the colander and adjust the heat so the water maintains a simmer. Cover and cook.

For soft-boiled eggs, steam for 6 minutes; for medium-hard, steam for 10 minutes; and for hard-boiled, steam for 12 minutes. When cooked, remove eggs to an ice-water bath, or run cold tap water over them to stop the cooking.

STEAM THE EGGS TO YOUR PREFERRED DONENESS

CLASSIC DEVILED EGGS

MAKES 24 DEVILED EGGS

NOTES / INGREDIENTS / METHOD:

Delicious deviled eggs combine something sour, something rich, and something spicy with creamy-smooth yolks and tender whites. The classic version reminds me of my childhood—and you can't go wrong with just a garnish of paprika and salt. Or add some caviar or salmon roe and chives for a sophisticated take on deviled eggs. Once you have the basics down, you could add any number of toppings to keep it interesting.

12 hard-boiled eggs (see page 101)
¼ cup mayonnaise
¼ cup crème fraîche
2 tablespoons Dijon mustard
Juice of ½ lemon
Kosher salt

OPTIONAL TOPPINGS
1 teaspoon smoked paprika
Flaky sea salt
1 ounce salmon roe or caviar
**¼ bunch of fresh chives,
    minced**

MAKE DEVILED EGGS MORE SOPHISTICATED WITH CAVIAR

Slice the eggs in half and remove the yolks to a food processor.

Season a bowl of cold water with as much salt as will dissolve in it. Rinse the egg whites of any remaining yolk in the salt water—this way, you season the eggs at the same time.

To the yolks in the food processor add the mayonnaise, crème fraîche, mustard, and lemon juice. Blend the mixture until it is completely smooth—you may have to add a few drops of water to loosen the mixture. Season to taste with salt.

Add the mixture to a piping bag, and pipe the filling into the egg white halves. If you prefer, use a teaspoon to fill the eggs; they'll look great either way.

Top the eggs as you wish, either with a sprinkle of smoked paprika and sea salt, or with a dollop of caviar and minced chives.

GARNISH THE EGGS WITH PAPRIKA BEFORE PUTTING THEM ON THE PLATTER

CAESAR SALAD "DEVILED EGGS"

MAKES 12
"DEVILED EGGS"

NOTES / INGREDIENTS / METHOD:

For this recipe, we totally rethought what "deviled eggs" means. The dressing we developed for the Caesar salad on page 223 was so tasty that we wanted to find another way to use it. Once we thought about what we had folded into the yolks to make a deviled-egg base, we asked, why not try folding in the dressing? Going down that path, we also figured that, instead of piping the yolk mixture into the egg whites, we could pipe it into small spears of crisp romaine and then crumble the egg white on top. This was such a hit that we added it to the menu at El Paseo shortly after developing the recipe.

2 slices sourdough bread
9 white Spanish anchovy fillets
Extra-virgin olive oil
6 hard-boiled eggs (see page 101)
⅓ cup Caesar Dressing (page 225)
5 tablespoons mayonnaise

2 tablespoons Dijon mustard
Juice of ½ lemon
Kosher salt
2 small hearts of baby romaine
Grated Parmesan cheese
Parsley leaves

Cut the bread slices into rough cubes, and add them and 3 anchovies to a food processor. Pulse to make "anchovy breadcrumbs." Coat a medium sauté pan with olive oil and set over medium heat. Add the breadcrumbs. Cook, stirring, until crisp, fragrant, and golden brown, about 5 minutes. Remove the breadcrumbs to paper towels.

Wipe out the food processor. Cut the eggs in half, and add the yolks to the food processor; set the whites aside. Add the dressing, mayonnaise, mustard, lemon juice, and a pinch of salt. Blend, and add more salt to taste.

Gently pull off the leaves from the romaine, then wash and blot dry with towels. Transfer the yolk mixture to a piping bag, and pipe onto the white centers of the romaine leaves. Cut the remaining 6 anchovy fillets in half, and top each leaf with an anchovy half. Sprinkle with the breadcrumbs.

Finely chop the egg whites, or push them through a sieve to grate them. Sprinkle them over the lettuce leaves. Top with some Parmesan and 1 parsley leaf per romaine spear. Serve immediately.

ANCHOVY BREADCRUMBS ARE THE CROUTONS FOR THIS "CAESAR"

PIPE THE FILLING INTO SMALL ROMAINE SPEARS

INFALLIBLE CHOCOLATE SOUFFLÉS

044

4

IT WAS IMPOSSIBLE NOT TO STICK A SPOON INTO THESE

↓

NOTES / INGREDIENTS / METHOD:

Soufflés seem like a huge deal to make and they often get a bad rap: you do a ton of work, but you don't know if the soufflé will rise in the oven, or, once it's done baking, if it will fall before you get it to the table. This method takes away that fear. Traditional soufflés have flour in the foundational béchamel, but these don't use any flour, making them both lighter in texture and also gluten free. Instead, xanthan gum is the stabilizer that helps contain the air bubbles, keeping the soufflé light and airy throughout. It also regulates moisture, so the eggs stay foamy and won't return to their liquid state. Those two factors combine to keep the soufflé from falling. You can find xanthan gum at most health food stores and larger grocery stores—it is an entirely natural product.

This recipe is for a chocolate soufflé, but there's a variation for an equally delicious raspberry soufflé that follows.

4 tablespoons (½ stick) unsalted butter, plus more for greasing ramekins

2 tablespoons sugar, plus more to coat ramekins

¼ teaspoon salt

2 cups chopped bittersweet chocolate

8 large eggs

½ teaspoon xanthan gum

Special equipment: four 6-ounce ramekins

Preheat the oven to 375°F. Grease the ramekins with some butter, then coat with some sugar, tapping out any excess.

Place 4 tablespoons butter, 2 tablespoons sugar, the salt, and chocolate in a pan over medium-low heat, and warm just until the mixture melts. Remove from the heat and stir very well so the chocolate is completely smooth. Let cool slightly.

Separate the eggs into two large, clean bowls. Lightly beat the egg yolks and add the chocolate, stirring well to incorporate the mixture and prevent the eggs from scrambling.

Using a balloon whisk or in a stand mixer, start to whisk the egg whites. Slowly incorporate the xanthan gum as you continue whisking the egg whites until you have stiff peaks.

Fold the egg whites into the chocolate mixture in three batches: the first third should be well blended, but fold in the remaining two batches more gently to retain the volume of the egg whites.

RECIPE CONTINUES

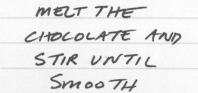

MELT THE CHOCOLATE AND STIR UNTIL SMOOTH

FOLD THE EGG WHITES INTO THE MELTED CHOCOLATE

Pour the batter into the ramekins, filling to the top. Using a knife, scrape the top of the batter to smooth the surface and remove any excess. With your forefinger and thumb, pinch the rim of each ramekin and run the edge of your thumb around the inside rim. (This trick makes the soufflés rise straight up while baking.)

Place the ramekins on a sheet pan or directly on the oven rack. Bake for 17 to 20 minutes, or until a gentle tap only jiggles the center of the soufflé. Serve immediately.

Infallible Raspberry Soufflé: Replace the chocolate and sugar with 2 cups of raspberry jam. Set the oven to 400°F, and proceed as above. (Note: this variation makes 5 soufflés, as the batter is lighter and the egg whites are able to retain more volume than the chocolate.)

RUN YOUR ~~HANDS~~
THUMB AROUND
THE INSIDE
RIM OF THE
RAMEKIN

THE FIVE-IN-ONE BAKING MIX

Breakfast is a big deal in our family. It's a special time when we're all together in the kitchen, before everyone breaks off to go their separate ways for the day. While I like to think it's all sunshine and rainbows, this time of the morning can also be a little chaotic, so time-savers are helpful.

My wife, Tolan, loves organic frozen whole wheat waffles for our kids; they're easy and she feels good about serving them. On weekend mornings when we have a little more time, though, it's nice to actually cook waffles or pancakes from scratch. The aroma of the pancakes wafting off the griddle is irresistible, no matter how old you are. But wouldn't it be great to have something in between frozen and from scratch? The nice thing about boxed mixes is their convenience, but the boxed mixes out there aren't necessarily nutritious. My rule of thumb is, if I can't pronounce an ingredient on the label, it's probably not good for me (or my family). So in the Test Kitchen, we set out to come up with our own version of a boxed mix, using ingredients we could pronounce and already had on hand.

After a full week of testing, we developed a dry mix that we think you'll love. It makes fluffy pancakes and light crispy waffles, but it also makes muffins, cake, and cookies. All you have to do is mix the dry ingredients and store the mix in your pantry for whenever you need it. Rather than fight the battle, let's make breakfast or snack time as easy and nutritious as possible.

RECIPES:

- FIVE-IN-ONE MIX 111

- MUFFINS 112

- PANCAKES 113

- WAFFLES 115

- CAKE 116

- COOKIES 118

THE
FIVE-IN-ONE
MIX MAKES
ENDLESS
VARIATIONS FOR
BREAKFAST AND DESSERT

FIVE-IN-ONE MIX
(FOR MUFFINS, PANCAKES, WAFFLES, CAKES, AND COOKIES)

NOTES / INGREDIENTS / METHOD:

Making Sunday-morning pancakes from a boxed mix might be easy, but it isn't necessarily nutritious. We were on a mission to find a natural way to create the same convenience without ingredients you can't pronounce, and we're thrilled with what we came up with. Our Five-in-One Mix makes pancakes, waffles, cakes, and muffins all from the same ingredients. (It makes cookies too; you just change the wet ingredients a bit.) And the possibilities are endless for variations on these; check out some of our favorites, and don't be afraid to try your own.

You can pre-combine the dry ingredients below and keep the mix in an airtight container indefinitely, adding the wet ingredients whenever you want to get baking.

SIFT TOGETHER
DRY INGREDIENTS

DRY INGREDIENTS
1½ cups all-purpose flour
½ cup cornstarch
2 teaspoons baking powder
1 teaspoon baking soda
1 teaspoon salt
½ cup sugar

WET INGREDIENTS
2 large eggs
2 cups buttermilk
1½ tablespoons vanilla extract
1 cup (2 sticks) unsalted butter, melted

Prepare the dry ingredients Sift together the flour, cornstarch, baking powder, baking soda, salt, and sugar into a large bowl.

Prepare the wet ingredients In a medium bowl, combine the eggs, buttermilk, vanilla, and melted butter, whisking as you add the butter.

Combine the ingredients Pour the wet ingredients into the dry ingredients, and whisk just until the batter comes together: you do not want to overmix.

Before using the batter, give it a little stir to let out any excess air.

DON'T OVERMIX THE BATTER ➔

MUFFINS

MAKES 8
STANDARD-SIZE
MUFFINS

HAVE A BATCH
ON HAND WHEN
FAMILY STAYS
WITH YOU

NOTES / INGREDIENTS / METHOD:

I try to make sure I always have a batch of muffins on hand when I have family visiting. It's a great way to take care of people who wake up at different times of the morning, as one by one they wander into the kitchen for some coffee and a bite to eat while others are still sleeping. Don't overmix the batter—otherwise, the muffins will get tough in baking.

1 recipe Five-in-One Mix (page 111)

Preheat the oven to 425°F. Grease an 8-cup muffin tin or place muffin liners into the cups. Spoon the batter into the muffin cups, filling to the top. Bake for 20 minutes, or until a toothpick inserted into the center of a muffin comes out clean.

Banana Bran Muffins: Substitute ½ cup bran for ½ cup of the dry ingredients. Substitute 1 cup well-mashed, very ripe banana for 1 cup of the buttermilk in the wet ingredients. Combine the wet and dry ingredients and bake as above.

Apple Pecan Muffins: Add 1 teaspoon ground cinnamon to the dry ingredients. Substitute 1 cup applesauce for 1 cup of the buttermilk in the wet ingredients. Combine the dry and wet ingredients, then fold in ½ cup chopped pecans and 1½ cups chopped apples into the batter. Pour into a 10-cup muffin tin and bake as above. Makes 10 muffins.

Cornbread Muffins: Substitute ½ cup fine-ground yellow cornmeal for ½ cup of the dry ingredients. Combine the dry and wet ingredients and bake as above.

PANCAKES

MAKES 12 PANCAKES

NOTES / INGREDIENTS / METHOD:

In the Florence house, pancakes are a regular occurrence. You can whip these up quickly, and adding extra toppings makes them even more special. My kids, Dorothy and Hayden, love helping me make them. Get the kids involved in stirring up the pancake batter—the more involved they are in the cooking process, the more likely they will be to gobble up whatever you are making. (But who wouldn't want pancakes anyway?)

1 recipe Five-in-One Mix (page 111)   **Vegetable oil, for cooking**

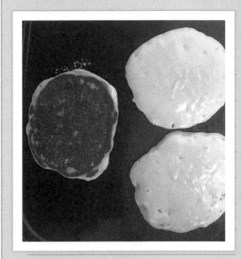

MY KIDS LOVE CHOCOLATE CHIPS IN THEIR PANCAKES

Lightly grease a griddle and put it over medium heat. When the griddle is hot, pour ⅓ cup portions of batter onto the griddle. When bubbles form on the surface and the bottoms are golden brown (about 4 minutes), flip and cook until set and golden. Lightly stir the batter before pouring each batch.

Lemon-Ricotta Pancakes: When mixing the wet ingredients, replace 1 cup of the buttermilk with 1 cup whole-milk ricotta (see page 57), and stir well to break it up. Add 1 tablespoon lemon zest and 1 tablespoon fresh lemon juice. Prepare the batter and cook as above.

Chocolate Chip or Butterscotch Pancakes: Add ½ cup chocolate or butterscotch chips to the batter. Cook as above.

Berry Pancakes: Add ¾ cup berries of your choice to the batter. If you use strawberries, slice them into quarters first. Cook as above.

WAFFLES

MAKES 6
WAFFLES

054–057

NOTES / INGREDIENTS / METHOD:

Weekday breakfasts at our house used to mean popping an organic frozen waffle into the toaster oven, but these are just as fast if you have the Five-in-One Mix ready to go. We used my mother-in-law's waffle iron for testing the original waffle recipes—and it sure got a lot of love!—but we loved using a Belgian waffle iron even more; it gives you waffles with great height.

1 recipe Five-in-One Mix (page 111)   Nonstick spray

Preheat the oven to 200°F. Heat a waffle iron to medium/medium-high, and coat with nonstick spray. Add 1 cup of batter to the waffle iron and smooth the batter before closing the iron. Cook the waffle until the steaming stops. Remove and keep cooked waffles in the oven on a rack while you finish making the rest.

SMOOTH THE BATTER BEFORE CLOSING THE WAFFLE IRON

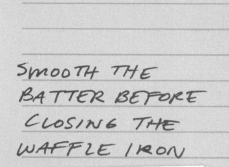

Bacon Waffles: In a pan over medium heat, render 4 ounces of bacon until crisp. Drain the bacon on paper towels and reserve the fat. When it's cool enough to handle, chop the bacon into bite-size pieces. Substitute 1 tablespoon bacon fat for 1 tablespoon butter in the waffles' wet ingredients. Blend the dry and wet ingredients, fold in the bacon pieces, and cook the waffles as above.

Pumpkin Waffles: Substitute 1 cup pureed pumpkin for 1 cup of the buttermilk in the wet ingredients. Add 1 teaspoon ground cinnamon, ½ teaspoon ground ginger, ¼ teaspoon ground cloves, and ¼ teaspoon grated nutmeg. Cook the waffles as above.

Banana Waffles: Substitute 1 cup very ripe mashed banana for 1 cup of the buttermilk in the wet ingredients. Cook the waffles as above.

I LOVE HOW MAPLE SYRUP POOLS IN THE CREVICES OF WAFFLES

CAKE

MAKES ONE
9-INCH CAKE

POUR THE BATTER
INTO A GREASED PAN

NOTES / INGREDIENTS / METHOD:

It's not a birthday without a birthday cake. This cake and its variations are just as easy to make as a box mix, but you can pronounce every ingredient that goes into them. Add frosting as desired: the lemon cake is fantastic with a cream cheese frosting.

1 recipe Five-in-One Mix (page 111)

Preheat the oven to 350°F. Grease a 9-inch cake pan, and pour in the batter. Bake for 30 to 35 minutes, or until a toothpick inserted into the center comes out clean.

DOUBLE THE RECIPE FOR TWO
LAYERS — OR SLICE ONE LAYER
IN HALF

Pineapple Upside-Down Cake

¼ cup (½ stick) unsalted butter
⅔ cup light brown sugar
9 pineapple slices

9 maraschino cherries
1 recipe Five-in-One Mix
(page 111)

Melt the butter in a saucepan over medium heat. Add the brown sugar and stir, cooking until the sugar dissolves and the mixture starts to bubble. Pour into the cake pan, then arrange the pineapple slices in the pan. Place a maraschino cherry in the center of each pineapple slice. Pour the batter into the cake pan, and bake as above. Cool the cake for 15 minutes, then flip onto a platter and serve.

Lemon Cake with Burst Berries

2 tablespoons grated lemon zest
2 tablespoons fresh lemon juice
¼ cup blackberries

¼ cup blueberries
1 recipe Five-in-One Mix
(page 111), made with ½ cup
less buttermilk

Combine the lemon zest, lemon juice, blackberries, and blueberries in a small bowl. Very lightly mash, just until the berries burst. Gently fold the berries into the batter and bake as above.

Coffee Cake

FOR THE CAKE
Dry ingredients for Five-in-One
Mix (page 111)
1 teaspoon ground cinnamon
2 large eggs
2 cups whole milk
1 tablespoon vanilla extract
¼ cup (½ stick) unsalted butter,
melted

FOR THE CRUMBLE
⅔ cup dry ingredients for
Five-in-One Mix (page 111)
⅔ cup brown sugar
1 teaspoon ground cinnamon
3 tablespoons unsalted butter,
cold

For the cake Whisk together the dry ingredients and cinnamon in a large bowl. In a medium bowl, combine the eggs, milk, vanilla, and melted butter, whisking as you add the butter. Pour the egg mixture into the dry ingredients, and whisk just until the batter comes together.

For the crumble Place the dry ingredients, brown sugar, cinnamon, and cold butter in a bowl and cut in the butter until you get a pea-sized crumb.

Pour half the batter into the cake pan, then sprinkle with half the crumble. Pour in the rest of the batter, then top with the remaining crumble. Bake as above.

062–065 COOKIES

MAKES 14 COOKIES

NOTES / INGREDIENTS / METHOD:

This is the only Five-in-One recipe that has a different wet-ingredient mix. Unlike the other baked goods, cookies require a little more sugar and less moisture to hold their texture and shape. We wanted a cookie with a nice crunch that reminded us of how we stole cookies from the cookie sheet when we were growing up. We have a few classic mix-ins, but you can make these your own by adding nuts or dried fruit.

½ cup (1 stick) unsalted butter, room-temperature soft
½ cup granulated sugar
½ cup brown sugar

1 large egg
1 teaspoon vanilla extract
Dry ingredients for one batch of Five-in-One Mix (page 111)

Cream the butter and both sugars in a large bowl until mixture gets light and fluffy. Add the egg and vanilla, and incorporate well. Add the dry ingredients and stir until the dough comes together. Place the dough on a piece of parchment paper, waxed paper, or plastic wrap, and shape into a log. Fold the paper over the dough, and continue tucking and rolling the log until you have a smooth roll about 3 inches in diameter. Refrigerate the wrapped log until it is firm, at least 30 minutes. (The cookies are actually best if you refrigerate the dough for 2 days before baking. This allows the starches to absorb the moisture from the wet ingredients, and makes a much richer-seeming cookie.)

Preheat the oven to 400°F. Remove the log from the refrigerator, and slice into cookies about ½ inch thick. Place on a cookie sheet lined with parchment paper and bake for 8 to 10 minutes, until the cookies are golden brown. Let the cookies cool slightly on the pan, then remove to a rack and cool completely.

ADD THE EGG AND VANILLA TO THE CREAMED BUTTER AND SUGAR

THE DOUGH WILL COME TOGETHER NICELY

PLACE THE DOUGH ONTO PARCHMENT PAPER

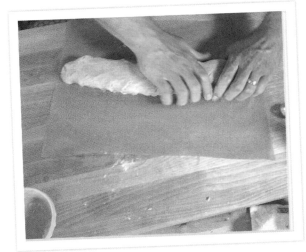

FORM THE DOUGH
INTO A LOG

TUCK AND ROLL
THE LOG USING
THE PARCHMENT...

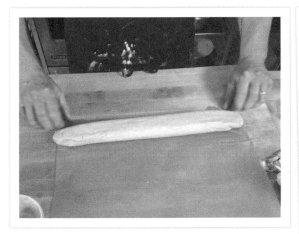

...UNTIL YOU
HAVE A SMOOTH
ROLL ABOUT
3 INCHES THICK

SLICE THE DOUGH
ABOUT 1/2 INCH THICK

RECIPE CONTINUES

FINISHED PRODUCT!

Chocolate Chip Cookies: Fold in 1 cup chocolate chips after the dough is mixed. Roll, chill, then slice and bake as above.

Oatmeal Cookies

½ cup (1 stick) unsalted butter, room-temperature soft
¼ cup granulated sugar
¾ cup brown sugar
1 egg

1 teaspoon vanilla extract
1 cup old-fashioned rolled oats
¼ teaspoon ground cinnamon
2 cups dry ingredients for Five-in-One Mix (page 111)

Cream together the butter and sugars, then add the egg and vanilla. Add the oats and cinnamon to the dry ingredients and stir into the butter-sugar mixture to form the dough. Roll, chill, then slice and bake as above.

Peanut Butter Cookies

¼ cup (1 stick) unsalted butter, room-temperature soft
1 cup light brown sugar
¼ cup peanut butter (or your favorite nut butter)

1 egg
1 teaspoon vanilla extract
2 cups dry ingredients for Five-in-One Mix (page 111)
Flaky sea salt

Cream the butter with the brown sugar, then add the peanut butter along with the egg and vanilla. Add the dry ingredients, and mix. Scoop tablespoons of the dough onto a parchment paper–lined cookie sheet and sprinkle with sea salt. Bake as above.

PASTA

It might be a universal truth that grandmothers are the best cooks around. Whether that belief stems from comforting memories of growing up or actual skill is yet to be determined, but I've learned a lot from the grandmothers I've encountered in my life. A few years ago, I was lucky enough to spend time in Campagna, Italy, learning to make pasta from a master—a woman who has been making pasta all her life and who probably has hand-cranked more pasta sheets in one week than I ever will in my lifetime.

The combinations of pastas and sauces are endless, and while pasta is a blank canvas, you want the dough to taste like something and have the right texture to hold up to a sauce. You want the sauce to stick to the pasta, and you want everything to look great on the plate. I love high-egg-yolk pasta dough: it gets this neon yellow that pops and shows its nutritional value. And making fresh pasta dough is very much worth the effort. It cooks in seconds, meaning you can have dinner on the table faster with fresh pasta than with dried. And a well-made pasta makes even the simplest sauce taste special. A big batch of fresh pasta and Herbed Pomodoro Sauce (page 141) on a Sunday can potentially carry you through the whole week. Actual results may vary, though, depending on how greedy the taste-testers are.

RECIPES:

- FRESH PASTA 123
- POLENTA GNOCCHI 128
- SLOW-COOKED BOLOGNESE SAUCE 132
- CARBONARA WITH CREAMY
  SCRAMBLED EGGS 134
- SPINACH-RICOTTA TORTELLINI 136
- SPAGHETTI AND MEATBALLS 138
- HERBED POMODORO SAUCE 141
- SPAGHETTI WITH SUMMER SQUASH
  AND PINE NUTS 142
- ONE-PAN LASAGNA 144

FRESH PASTA

NOTES / INGREDIENTS / METHOD:

Fresh pasta dough is the ultimate blank canvas for thousands of delicious dinners. But at the end of the day, good pasta dough is all about structure. Semolina is a durum wheat that brings flavor to the pasta but is too coarse on its own, while all-purpose flour provides a silky texture with little nutritional value; we found that using both gave us a perfect balance. After testing a few recipes, we ended up with a 50:50 blend of all-purpose flour and semolina, with a high egg-yolk content. A splash of vinegar helps the gluten develop and preserves the bright yellow color in the egg yolks. This dough works beautifully for everything from spaghetti to lasagna to tortellini.

¾ cup all-purpose flour
¾ cup semolina flour
12 large egg yolks
2 tablespoons extra-virgin olive oil

¼ cup whole milk
1½ teaspoons salt
1½ teaspoons white vinegar

Add the two flours to a blender and blend until very fine in texture. You may have to do this in batches. Reserve ¼ cup of the flour, and set the rest on a clean, flat surface.

Mound the flour in the center of the work surface. Using your fingers, create a well in the center about 6 inches in diameter. Add the yolks to the well, then add the olive oil, milk, salt, and vinegar. Using a fork, puncture the yolks and mix the wet ingredients together, gradually bringing the flour into the egg mixture from the inside wall of the well. (You could also do this with a stand mixer fitted with the hook attachment; first mix the wet ingredients and then add the flour and salt.)

Once the eggs are integrated, use your hands to combine them with the rest of the flour and knead it. Don't worry if it looks dry; a ball will naturally come together as you work it. Continue kneading the dough until it comes together in a smooth ball. Cover the dough with plastic wrap and let it rest for at least 30 minutes to relax the gluten.

RECIPE CONTINUES

MIX THE WET INGREDIENTS TOGETHER IN THE WELL

KNEAD THE DOUGH TOGETHER UNTIL IT'S A SMOOTH BALL

Set up either a hand-crank pasta roller or the pasta attachment of a stand mixer. With a rolling pin, roll the dough out into a rough square about twice the width of the opening of your pasta roller. Fold the square in half, and roll the rectangle lengthwise until it's about ½ inch thick. This should give you a thick sheet that will fit into the pasta roller.

Adjust your pasta rollers to the widest setting and crank the dough through. Dust the rolled-out sheet with flour so that it moves smoothly through the machine.

Work the dough through the sequence of settings so that the pasta builds good structure and doesn't tear as it thins. Tighten the rollers to the next setting and crank the dough through, dusting with more flour if it feels tacky. Repeat the process until the dough is thin enough to see your hands through it. If the dough sheet gets too long to handle comfortably, cut it in half across the middle and roll out the sheets separately. The pasta dough is now ready for cutting into desired shapes.

Lasagna: Cut the thin sheets of dough to your desired size, usually 2 or 3 inches wide and 9 inches long.

Pappardelle: Cut the thin sheets of dough into 7- to 9-inch-long sheets. Roll the sheets into a loose log so that slicing the log will result in long strips. Cut into 1-inch-wide strips. Unfurl the strips and lay them out flat on a sheet pan and dust with flour. Serve with Slow-Cooked Bolognese Sauce (page 132).

Tortellini, Ravioli, and Other Stuffed Pastas: Dough for stuffed shapes should be a bit thinner than for other pastas, because they will be folded over on themselves. After you get the pasta to the point where you can see through it, crank it through a few more times on an even thinner setting, then use a circular biscuit cutter or knife to cut the dough before filling the pasta. Use in Spinach-Ricotta Tortellini (page 136).

Spaghetti: Use the spaghetti cutter attachment on your pasta machine to cut the dough into long strands. Dust the pasta with flour as it comes out of the machine so the strands do not stick together. Use in Spaghetti and Meatballs (page 138).

ROLL THE DOUGH THROUGH THE SEQUENCE of SETTINGS

YOU CAN MAKE DIFFERENT CUTS of PASTA FOR DIFFERENT USES

THE GREAT

1# Fresh Pasta

1# Dry Pasta

WE SET 1 POUND OF OUR FRESH PASTA AGAINST 1 POUND OF DRIED TO SEE WHICH WOULD BE ON ~~THE~~ THE TABLE FIRST

FRESH PASTA RACE

A watched pot never boils . . . and even when you *aren't* watching, it still seems to take forever. So we asked ourselves: Why is dried pasta a convenience food but homemade fresh pasta is thought of as a huge project? We made a bet in the Test Kitchen that we could make and cook fresh pasta in less time than it takes to bring water to a boil and cook dried pasta. Is dried pasta more convenient than fresh pasta is tasty?

We set two large pots of salted water over high heat to bring them to a boil, then we mixed, rolled, and cut fresh pasta dough (though, to be fair, we skipped the step of resting the dough). Fourteen minutes later, the water in both pots was boiling, and our fresh pasta was ready to go. But here's the thing: the dried pasta took 12 minutes to cook, while our fresh pasta was out of the water in 90 seconds. With dried pasta, that's almost half an hour before dinner is on the table, whereas fresh pasta gets it there faster and is more nutritious, with a more subtle texture and richer flavor.

Granted, we've made enough fresh pasta to be pretty quick at it, but considering how fast it cooks, you'll still have a good head start over that box of spaghetti.

POLENTA GNOCCHI

4

NOTES / INGREDIENTS / METHOD:

I always want everyone who comes into my restaurants to have a great meal, and with gluten intolerance affecting more and more people, we need to make adjustments to be conscious of people's needs. Traditional potato gnocchi includes flour, but these gnocchi are made with polenta, which is naturally gluten-free. Kneading and cooling the dough make it easier to shape into gnocchi. My wife, Tolan, loves the idea of making gnocchi, but like many, she finds it takes too many steps. But with this recipe, all you need is one saucepan and a flat surface to bring this comforting dish to life.

    Unlike potato gnocchi, these gnocchi don't need to be boiled before serving. A quick sear in a pan or a quick trip in the oven, and you're good to go with a sauce of your choice. Following the basic recipe are two of our favorite ways to serve these gnocchi.

1 quart whole milk
2 rosemary sprigs
2 thyme sprigs
4 fresh sage leaves
6 garlic cloves
1 cup corn flour (extra-fine polenta), plus more for dusting (see Note) ★

5 tablespoons unsalted butter
⅓ cup freshly grated Parmesan cheese
1 teaspoon grated nutmeg
½ teaspoon salt
3 large egg yolks
1 teaspoon honey

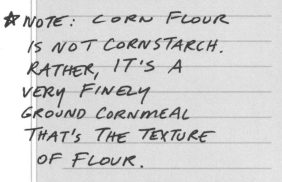

★ NOTE: CORN FLOUR IS NOT CORNSTARCH. RATHER, IT'S A VERY FINELY GROUND CORNMEAL THAT'S THE TEXTURE OF FLOUR.

Pour the milk into a medium saucepan and add the rosemary, thyme, sage, and garlic. Over medium heat, warm the mixture to 170°F, or until bubbles form around the rim of the pan. Remove from the heat, then pull out and discard the herbs and garlic.

Slowly "rain" the corn flour into the milk, stirring continuously so that it doesn't clump up. Put the pan back over medium heat, and stir constantly. Allow the mixture to come to a simmer; it will start to thicken from the natural starch in the corn. Cook the polenta until it gets creamy, like thick pancake batter, adding more milk or water if necessary.

Remove the saucepan from the heat, and add the butter, cheese, nutmeg, and salt, and stir for a few minutes to help the mixture cool down. Add the egg yolks and honey and stir. The residual heat will cook the yolks.

COOK THE POLENTA UNTIL THICK

When the batter is cool enough to handle, dust a surface with some corn flour. Transfer the mixture to the work surface, and dust with more corn flour. Knead the dough, adding more corn flour as necessary, until it is no longer tacky. Spread the dough out into a 1-inch-thick disk. Let the dough cool for a few minutes, until just warm.

Wet your hands with a bit of water so the dough doesn't stick to them. Roll the dough into ½-inch-thick logs, and cut into 1-inch-long pieces. Roll the dough pieces between your palms to make into balls. Then, roll the dough balls on the tines of a fork to make indentations in the dough. Sear in a hot sauté pan with some olive oil or butter, or broil, and serve with a sauce of your choice. Two of our favorites are below.

RECIPE CONTINUES

ROLL THE DOUGH INTO LOGS, THEN CUT INTO PIECES

Gnocchi Pomodoro: Preheat the oven to broil. Add 1 cup Herbed Pomodoro Sauce (page 141) to the bottom of a baking dish. Place the gnocchi on top of the sauce. Drizzle with extra-virgin olive oil. Grate fresh Parmesan over the gnocchi. Break a ball of burrata cheese into small pieces and place in between the gnocchi. Broil for 3 to 5 minutes, until the cheese is melted and the gnocchi are toasted on the top. Finish with fresh basil, marjoram, parsley leaves, and more freshly grated Parmesan.

BROILING ADDS A NICE CRUNCH

Gnocchi Bolognese: Coat a large sauté pan with olive oil and heat over medium-high heat until oil is shimmering. Pan-fry the gnocchi until they are golden brown on both sides. Plate the gnocchi with Slow-Cooked Bolognese Sauce (page 132) and finish with extra-virgin olive oil, grated Parmesan, and fried herbs (from the sauce recipe).

SLOW-COOKED BOLOGNESE SAUCE

068

MAKES 5 QUARTS

FRYING THE HERBS MAKES A HUGE DIFFERENCE — AND IT'S SO SIMPLE

NOTES / INGREDIENTS / METHOD:

This is one of the sauces that anyone should know how to make. You have to have a few great standby recipes under your belt, and this creamy, deeply flavored sauce goes miles in the kitchen. In Italy, I learned that using three types of meat makes a huge difference, and I also use this base in my meatballs (see page 138). The beef brings flavor, the veal provides a soft texture, and the pork adds the fat. The recipe is actually fairly simple, even though it does take some time to build the deep, meaty flavors and smooth texture. But the time is worth it; you end up with a ton of sauce for dinner, plus leftovers for days.

Serve this sauce with Polenta Gnocchi (page 128) or Pappardelle (see page 124), with the fried herbs as a garnish.

2 carrots
5 celery ribs
1 onion
6 garlic cloves
1 cup dried porcini mushrooms
About 1 cup extra-virgin olive oil
6 sage leaves
2 rosemary sprigs
2 thyme sprigs
2 oregano sprigs
Kosher salt
1½ pounds ground beef

1½ pounds ground pork
1 pound ground veal
Freshly ground black pepper
2 (28-ounce) cans whole San Marzano tomatoes
1 quart whole milk
½ bottle red wine
1 cinnamon stick
⅓ cup freshly grated Parmesan cheese
½ cup chopped parsley
3 tablespoons heavy cream
Juice of 1 lemon

Roughly chop the carrots, celery, and onion and add to a food processor. Add the garlic and dried mushrooms to the food processor and grind the ingredients, occasionally pushing down any bits at the sides of the processor with a spoon—you want a smooth texture, so the vegetables will add body to the sauce. Add ¼ cup of the olive oil to help the process. (If you'd like a rougher texture, you can hand chop the vegetables very finely, then combine with the olive oil.)

Heat ½ cup of the olive oil over medium-high heat in a large, heavy-bottomed pot. Add the sage, rosemary, thyme, and oregano to the oil and lightly fry the herbs until just crisp but still green. Remove the fried herbs and reserve. Now, you have an herb-infused olive oil and also a garnish for the finished sauce.

Pour the vegetable puree into the infused oil, being careful not to splash yourself. Season with a generous pinch of salt and sauté the vegetables; you want to cook out the water to concentrate the flavors and to caramelize the mixture. Cook, stirring regularly with a wooden spoon, until the vegetables are nicely browned, then transfer them to a plate.

Add 2 tablespoons of the oil to the pot, raise the heat to high, and when the oil shimmers, add the beef, pork, and veal. Season the meat with salt and pepper and break it up with the spoon so that it covers the bottom of the pot. Once the meat browns on the bottom, stir and flip it so each side of the meat can touch the bottom and sear. Once the meat is deeply, evenly browned, add the vegetables back to the pot and stir to combine. Add the canned tomatoes (leave them whole). Stir in the milk, red wine, and a few generous pinches of salt. The acid from the red wine will curdle the milk at first, but as the sauce cooks together, the texture will smooth out. Add the cinnamon stick.

When the sauce comes to a boil, turn it down to a very low, lazy bubbling simmer and cook, partially covered, for 3 hours. It will become nice and creamy. Remove the cinnamon stick, and finish with the Parmesan, parsley, and a drizzle of the oil. Add the cream and season to taste with salt, pepper, and lemon juice.

SAN MARZANOS ARE PICKED AT PEAK RIPENESS

THE PERFECT COMFORT FOOD

069

CARBONARA WITH CREAMY SCRAMBLED EGGS

4

NOTES / INGREDIENTS / METHOD:

The usual method of making pasta carbonara involves tossing cooked pasta with a mixture of raw eggs, crisp pork jowl or belly, salt, pepper, and Parmesan, with the egg cooking in the residual heat of the pasta. We made a version that cooks the eggs first, taking away any anxiety people might have about serving raw eggs; but we're also amping up the dish with herbs and custardy scrambled eggs. This is a classic pairing with spaghetti, but we love the carbonara preparation with the Spinach-Ricotta Tortellini (page 136).

4 bacon slices
3 garlic cloves
3 thyme sprigs
8 large eggs plus 4 yolks
4 tablespoons (½ stick) unsalted butter
1 cup heavy cream

½ cup freshly grated Parmesan cheese, plus more for serving
Kosher salt
Freshly ground black pepper
1 batch Spinach-Ricotta Tortellini (page 136), or 1 pound of Fresh Pasta (page 123)

Cut the bacon into ¼-inch sticks and fry in a large skillet over medium-low heat. Crush the garlic with the side of your knife and add, whole, to the bacon along with the thyme sprigs to infuse the bacon fat with flavor. Cook until the bacon is rendered but not quite crisp. Remove the thyme and garlic, but keep the bacon in the pan off the heat.

Bring a large pot of generously salted water to a boil.

Add the eggs, yolks, and butter to a medium saucepan (preferably nonstick) as the bacon is frying. Barely heat the pan over low heat with the eggs, then pop the yolks and stir constantly with a rubber spatula until the eggs thicken a bit. Keep a close eye on the eggs: once they start to cook, they will cook very quickly. Low and slow is the key to a luxurious texture. The temperature of coddled eggs is 149°F; you want this egg sauce to get to 145°F. The eggs will be thick and custardy, but still south of scrambled eggs.

Add the cream and ½ cup Parmesan, and season with salt and pepper, then stir to combine. Take the pan off the heat, but keep stirring it occasionally so the eggs don't overcook around the edges.

While the eggs are resting off the heat, cook the tortellini or pasta in the boiling water until al dente. Add a few tablespoons of the pasta water to the eggs, drain the pasta, and combine with the eggs back in the pasta pot, off the heat. Add the bacon and its fat, and stir together for the sauce to come together and thicken. The sauce and pasta should be very warm, but not screaming hot. If it's too cool, stir it over a low flame until hot.

Plate the pasta, top with freshly ground black pepper and more Parmesan cheese, and serve immediately.

MAKING YOUR OWN FILLED PASTA IS EASY BUT LOOKS IMPRESSIVE

SPINACH-RICOTTA TORTELLINI

4 to 6

NOTES / INGREDIENTS / METHOD:

Filled pastas can have an endless array of shapes, fillings, and sauces—we could go on for days about the possibilities. This is a classic spinach-ricotta filling that can be used in tortellini or, even more easily, in ravioli. Keep in mind that for filled pastas, you are doubling the dough on itself when you fold it, so the sheets need to be thinner than for pastas like pappardelle. Shaping tortellini might seem intimidating, but with a few quick folds you'll be done in no time. I love this with carbonara sauce (see page 134); it gets into the folds of the pasta to make each bite delicious.

1¼ pounds fresh spinach
1 cup fresh ricotta (see page 57)
Zest of 2 lemons
1 teaspoon fresh lemon juice
¼ cup freshly grated Parmesan cheese
2 eggs

½ teaspoon grated nutmeg
Kosher salt
Freshly ground pepper
6 sheets Fresh Pasta,
    each about 6 x 12 inches
    (page 123)
Cornmeal, for sprinkling

RUN A PARING KNIFE AROUND A JAR IF YOU DON'T HAVE A PASTRY CUTTER

Set a large pot of salted water to boil, and wash the spinach until it's free of any grit or dirt. Blanch the spinach until wilted and tender, a minute or so, and then remove it to a bowl of ice water to cool. Drain the spinach and squeeze it until you've gotten all the excess water out. Chop it fine.

In a medium bowl, combine the spinach with the ricotta, lemon zest, lemon juice, Parmesan, one of the eggs, and the nutmeg. Season to taste with salt and pepper. Transfer the mixture to a piping bag.

Beat the remaining egg in a small bowl with 1 tablespoon of water to make an egg wash. Cut the sheets of pasta into circles using a 2¾-inch pastry cutter, and working in batches of six, brush the top half of each circle with egg wash. Pipe a bit of the filling about the size of a quarter into the center of the circle. Fold the pasta circle in half upwards and gently press to seal so you have a semicircle with the straight edge on the bottom.

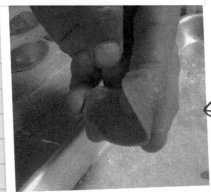

BRING THE CORNERS TOGETHER AND PRESS TO SEAL

Dab egg wash on the bottom corners. Bring the corners together and gently press them together to seal. Fold the top down toward the back of the pasta (this is called the Pope's Hat), and place the finished tortellini on a dish sprinkled with cornmeal.

When ready to serve, cook the pasta in boiling, generously salted water for about 4 minutes, until they all float. Drain, and serve with the sauce of your choice.

071   SPAGHETTI AND MEATBALLS

10 to 12

NOTES / INGREDIENTS / METHOD:

Meatballs hold a special place in people's hearts, as there is usually a grandmother involved in the story. I once worked with a woman in Campagna, Italy, and she taught me a great technique for making juicy, flavorful meatballs. The first key is using pork for fat, veal for texture, and beef for flavor, just like we did in the Slow-Cooked Bolognese Sauce (page 132). The second key is to bind them with milk-soaked bread—this adds moisture. The third key is to shallow-fry the meatballs to brown the surface evenly and keep them round, then to cook and cool them in the sauce to marry the flavors.

½ large onion
5 garlic cloves
½ cup parsley leaves
Extra-virgin olive oil
4 cups bread pieces, in ¼-inch pieces (from 1 loaf)
1 cup whole milk
1½ pounds ground beef
1½ pounds ground pork
1½ pounds ground veal

⅓ cup freshly grated Parmesan cheese, plus more for serving
1 teaspoon kosher salt
Freshly ground black pepper
Grapeseed or vegetable oil, for frying
1 recipe Herbed Pomodoro Sauce (page 141)
3 pounds freshly made spaghetti (see page 124)
6 basil leaves

Finely chop the onion, garlic, and parsley, but keep separate. Coat a medium sauté pan with olive oil and set over medium-high heat. Add the onion and garlic and cook, stirring occasionally, until the onion softens and browns a little. Add the parsley and 1 tablespoon of olive oil, and remove from the heat.

Place the bread in a bowl, cover it with the milk, and let it absorb for a few minutes. Squish it until it becomes uniform in texture.

Stir the parsley-onion mixture into the bread mixture, and then add the beef, pork, veal, ⅓ cup cheese, the salt, and a few grinds of black pepper. Lightly mix it with a spoon just enough to combine the elements; overworking the mixture will make the meatballs tough.

Using a small ice-cream scoop, portion out the mixture and roll between your hands to form balls. Each meatball should be about the size of a golf ball. It helps if you have a bit of water on your hands to keep the meat from sticking as you roll the meat into balls.

FLAVOR WITH ONION, GARLIC, AND PARSLEY

Heat 1 inch of grapeseed oil in a large, deep-sided sauté pan or pot over medium-high heat. When the oil is at 375°F, shallow-fry the meatballs in batches until browned. Remove the meatballs to a paper towel–lined sheet pan.

Bring the sauce to a simmer over medium heat in a wide pan. Add the meatballs, gently tossing to coat them in the sauce. Cover the pot with a lid or foil and simmer gently for 45 minutes. (If you're not serving right away, let the meatballs cool in the sauce.)

While the meatballs simmer, bring a large pot of generously salted water to a boil over high heat. When the meatballs are almost ready, cook the fresh spaghetti in the boiling water until it's tender but al dente, about 90 seconds.

Place the pasta in a bowl and add the meatball sauce, along with some Parmesan and the basil leaves, and stir. Transfer the pasta to a serving dish, top with the meatballs, add some more Parmesan, and drizzle on a bit of olive oil. Serve immediately.

FRYING MEATBALLS SETS THEIR SHAPE

SOUS — VIDE MEATBALLS

After making a meatball mixture we loved, we were curious about how we might cook them. Are they better braised or cooked sous-vide?

We cooked both versions in Herbed Pomodoro Sauce (page 141) for about 45 minutes, then allowed the meatballs to cool in the sauce so they would continue to absorb flavor. The next day, we reheated both sets to do a final taste. The braised meatballs were delicious, but the sous-vide meatballs were noticeably moister and held on more to the flavors of both the meat and the sauce. By cooking the meatballs sous-vide, no moisture was lost to evaporation, nor were the juices leached into the sauce as the meatballs cooked, so we ended up with very silky, delicately structured meatballs.

If you have a sous-vide setup at home, try this: After the quick shallow-fry step in our meatball recipe (see page 139), transfer the meatballs to half-gallon sous-vide bags and add some sauce. (Each bag will likely hold 9 meatballs and 1½ to 2 cups of sauce.) Seal the bags with a vacuum sealer. Place the bags in an immersion circulator set at 145°F (63°C), and cook for 45 minutes. If necessary, you can cool the bags down and reheat them the next day at the same temperature for about 10 minutes. You can let the meatballs stay at this temperature until you serve them.

HERBED POMODORO SAUCE

NOTES / INGREDIENTS / METHOD:

In many of my recipes, I start out by frying herbs in olive oil to infuse the oil with flavor. This step elevates what would otherwise be a simple tomato sauce to a whole new level. For most of the year, outside of tomato season, we like to use canned San Marzano tomatoes. They are a rich Italian variety, picked at the height of ripeness, then steamed and canned immediately. You can use this sauce for a number of recipes, including Spaghetti and Meatballs (page 138) or Polenta Gnocchi (page 128).

1 onion
4 garlic cloves
2 (28-ounce) cans whole San
   Marzano tomatoes
½ cup extra-virgin olive oil, plus
   more for drizzling
2 oregano sprigs

2 rosemary sprigs
2 marjoram sprigs
Kosher salt
Freshly ground black pepper
½ teaspoon dried red chile flakes
10 basil leaves, torn

Dice the onion and mince the garlic. Hand-crush the tomatoes in a large mixing bowl, squeezing slowly so they don't explode. You could also use an immersion blender or leave them whole, but hand-crushing results in a rustic texture.

Add ½ cup olive oil to a large saucepan over medium heat. Add the oregano, rosemary, and marjoram to infuse the oil with the herbs as it heats up. Once they are crisp and the oil is hot, remove the herbs and discard.

START BY INFUSING OIL WITH FRESH HERBS

Add the onion and garlic to the oil along with a pinch of salt. Cook the onion down until it is translucent but not yet browned. Pour the tomatoes and their juices into the pot, bring them to a boil, and turn the heat down to a simmer. Season with salt and pepper.

After about 30 minutes, the acidity of the tomatoes will drop and the moisture will evaporate, leaving you with a sweet, rich sauce. Adjust the seasoning with salt, pepper, and chile flakes, and drizzle with more olive oil. Top with the torn basil leaves.

SIMMER FOR ABOUT 30 MINUTES →

SPAGHETTI WITH SUMMER SQUASH AND PINE NUTS

NOTES / INGREDIENTS / METHOD:

I'm a big fan of letting produce shine, and living in California has definitely driven that idea home. This sauce relies on pureed summer squash for its fresh taste and color. By reserving some cooked pieces of squash and frying up a few squash blossoms, we highlight the abundance of squash in a few different ways. It's also quick to get the dish onto the dinner table, and this is a perfect use for this beautiful, healthful summer vegetable.

AN ELEGANT
SUMMER
DINNER

1 large onion
2 medium yellow summer squash
2 medium pattypan squash
2 medium zucchini
2 garlic cloves
Extra-virgin olive oil
Kosher salt
Freshly ground black pepper

2 tablespoons pine nuts
Grapeseed or vegetable oil, for frying
4 squash blossoms
1 pound spaghetti (see page 124)
Grated Parmesan cheese
6 fresh basil leaves

Chop the onion into 1-inch pieces, then cut the summer squash, pattypan squash, and zucchini into ¼-inch rounds. Mince the garlic. Generously coat a medium saucepan with some olive oil and set over medium heat. When the oil shimmers, add the vegetables to the pan with a generous pinch of salt and pepper. Cook, stirring occasionally as the vegetables sweat down. Once they are tender but not falling apart, add three-fourths of the vegetables to a blender and reserve the rest in a bowl in a warm place. Blend the squash until smooth, season with salt and pepper to taste, and return to the saucepan. Keep over low heat so it stays warm.

While the squash is cooking, set a large pot of water to boil over high heat and season it generously with salt.

Toast the pine nuts in a tall saucepan over medium heat until aromatic, then remove and set aside. Heat 2 inches of grapeseed oil in that saucepan to 360°F over medium-high heat. Fry the squash blossoms—two at a time if all four don't fit comfortably in the pan—until golden brown. Drain on a paper towel–lined plate and season with salt and pepper.

Cook the spaghetti in the boiling salted water for about 45 seconds, until al dente. Drain, then drizzle olive oil over the pasta. Toss the cooked spaghetti with the blended squash. Top with Parmesan cheese, a drizzle of olive oil, and salt to taste.

Plate the pasta in a serving dish. Top with the remaining vegetables, fried squash blossoms, and pine nuts. Garnish with torn fresh basil leaves and serve with additional Parmesan cheese.

USE A VARIETY OF SQUASH FOR THIS

PUREED VEGETABLES ARE A HEALTHY, FAST SAUCE

ONE-PAN LASAGNA

NOTES / INGREDIENTS / METHOD:

Usually when you make lasagna, you have to boil the noodles, assemble the layers, and cook the dish. Then, when you finally cut into it and put it on the plate, it looks like goop. It's just not worth the time. In this version, though, we press sheets of uncooked fresh pasta into a pot of sauce, eliminating the need to carefully add each layer and letting the pasta cook directly in the flavorful sauce. The pan goes from the stove to the oven to the table, making it a fast dinner and easy cleanup, too. We use ground beef in this recipe, but you could substitute ground turkey or chicken, if desired.

2 carrots, cut into quarters
2 garlic cloves
1 onion, quartered
Extra-virgin olive oil
1¼ (28-ounce) cans San Marzano tomatoes (36 ounces total)
1 pound ground meat (beef, turkey, or chicken)
Kosher salt

Freshly ground black pepper
8 sheets Fresh Pasta (page 123) or instant-cook, 4 x 8 inches
3 ounces fresh spinach leaves
1 pint fresh ricotta (see page 57)
8 ounces fresh mozzarella, cubed
⅓ cup freshly grated Parmesan cheese

FINELY CHOP THE VEGETABLES

Add the carrots, garlic, and onion to a food processor and process until very finely chopped.

Place a 10-inch oven-safe sauté pan with tall, straight sides over medium heat. Coat the bottom of the pan with some olive oil, and add the carrot mixture. Cook, stirring occasionally, until the vegetables are soft and well caramelized. While the vegetables cook, pour the tomatoes and their juice into the food processor and puree.

RECIPE CONTINUES

SIMMER SAUCE
FOR 20 MINUTES

Remove the caramelized vegetables to a bowl and add another 2 tablespoons of olive oil to the pan. Increase the heat to medium-high, and when the oil is shimmering, add the meat to the pan, breaking it up with a wooden spoon. Season generously with salt and pepper, and let it sear until well browned. Add the pureed tomatoes, another few generous pinches of salt and pepper, and stir. Bring the meat and tomatoes to a simmer, and simmer gently for 20 minutes to marry the flavors.

Meanwhile, preheat the oven to 350°F.

After the sauce has cooked, reduce the heat to low. Place a sheet of pasta over the sauce and push down with the spoon so the pasta submerges. Use a wiggling motion so that all the meat doesn't get pushed down to the bottom. Continue placing layers of pasta in the pot and pushing them down, creating layers of pasta and meat sauce within the pan. The pasta will cook in the sauce, thickening it. When the pasta is all in the pot, add the spinach on top. Dollop the ricotta over the spinach, and then add the mozzarella. Top with Parmesan cheese, a drizzle of olive oil, and a pinch of salt.

Place the pan in the oven and bake, uncovered, until the cheese is melted and bubbling, about 25 minutes. Serve immediately.

THREE DIFFERENT
CHEESES?
YES, PLEASE.

PORK CHOPS

We've all heard the saying "Give a man a fish and you feed him for a day; teach him to fish and you feed him for a lifetime." Part of the *Inside the Test Kitchen* philosophy is to empower home cooks by explaining the science of what happens in the kitchen. Anyone can replicate the steps in a recipe, but when you understand the reasons things happen, you will be able to do more than follow directions.

When we embarked on "Pork Week," we knew we needed to spend time on pork chops. Getting dinner on the table during the week can entail some work, but breaking bread with the family is so important that the effort is worthwhile. Studies have shown that families that eat dinner together eat more healthfully, have children who do better in school, and have teenagers who are less likely to smoke, drink, or do drugs. Pork chops are a great weeknight dinner option, with endless variations.

Having the pork supplied by the nearby Marin Sun Farms, we were off to a good start; what we needed was to come up with a few variations that would be memorable. We started by testing whether the result of brining the pork chops was worth the effort. The answer was a resounding yes; but rather than developing a brine with flavors that cover up the pork, we turned up the volume on its natural flavors. Then we added some of our favorite combinations of sides and accompaniments. Once you have the brining step down, you can add whatever flavors you want, or even pair the brined and seared pork chops with other recipes in this book.

RECIPES:

- ALMOND MILK BRINE   150

- SEARED BRINED PORK CHOPS   151

- PORK CHOPS WITH CARAMELIZED
  BANANAS AND HERB AIOLI   152

- PORK CHOPS WITH CREAMED KALE
  AND FENNEL-APRICOT SALAD   155

- PORK CHOPS WITH SEARED
  SUMMER SQUASH, TOMATO, AND
  BLACK OLIVE TAPENADE   156

- PORK SCHNITZEL WITH
  SAGE AND CAPERS   158

- PORK CHOPS WITH ROASTED APPLE,
  BRUSSELS SPROUTS, AND BACON   160

TEST: # BRINED VS. UNBRINED PORK TEST

We wanted to test the value of brining pork: does it really make the meat that much better? So we tasted both a brined and unbrined pork chop side by side and found that, hands down, the brined version was far more tender and juicy.

But what about flavor? Most brines are simply a mixture of salt, sugar, and water, but we wanted to develop a brine that really highlights the flavors of pork. We tasted an unseasoned pork chop to understand the nuances of pork flavor, just as you would a new wine. As we ate, we wrote down the flavors that we were tasting:

— IRON / LIVER

— SUGAR

— FOREST FLOOR / GRASS

— EUCALYPTUS

— CARAMEL

— ALMOND

— SAGE

— WOOD

— HAZELNUT

We then used these flavor profiles to create a brine that would maximize those flavors we found naturally in pork. We love what we've come up with (see page 150); it's our go-to pork brine from now on.

075

ALMOND MILK BRINE

NOTES / INGREDIENTS / METHOD:

A brine is a salt solution that penetrates the protein in a meat and replaces the natural liquid with the brine flavors, creating a juicy piece of meat that's seasoned from the inside out. Often, though, a flavored brine can cover up the meat instead of letting it shine. This brine adds brown sugar and nutty and forest herbal notes to highlight the natural flavors of pork.

1 quart unsweetened almond milk
¼ cup salt
⅓ cup brown sugar
2 fresh sage leaves

1 thyme sprig
½ bay leaf
1 tablespoon dried porcini
**   mushroom pieces**

Heat the almond milk, salt, brown sugar, sage, thyme, bay leaf, and mushrooms in a large saucepan over medium-low heat. You do not need to boil the liquid; just heat it enough so the salt and sugar dissolve. Stir with a whisk, then transfer to a bowl. Let cool down completely.

THIS BRINE
HIGHLIGHTS THE
NATURAL FLAVORS
IN PORK

SEARED BRINED PORK CHOPS

NOTES / INGREDIENTS / METHOD:

This is my favorite way of cooking pork chops. It's fast and gives fantastic results. The sugars from the brine caramelize a bit when the pork cooks, contributing a slight crispy edge. You can serve this master pork chop recipe with a Caesar salad (see page 223) or with the four recipes that follow. You can either prepare the sides ahead of time, keep the pork chops warm in a 200°F oven while you prepare the sides, or cook the pork chops and the sides simultaneously to ensure you have warm pork chops on the dinner table.

1 quart **Almond Milk Brine** (opposite)
4 **(1-inch-thick) pork chops**

Grapeseed or vegetable oil
Kosher salt
Freshly ground black pepper

THE BRINE'S SUGARS WILL CARAMELIZE IN THE PAN

Soak the pork chops in the brine in the refrigerator for at least 30 minutes and up to 1 hour. Remove from the brine and allow the chops to come to room temperature, then pat dry with paper towels. As they have been brined, there is no need to season the chops before cooking.

Heat a heavy sauté pan over medium-high heat. Add enough oil to generously slick the bottom of the pan. When the oil shimmers, carefully add as many pork chops as will fit comfortably in the pan. Sear the pork chops for about 5 minutes on each side, so that they have a nice, even brown color and are cooked to medium. (If using a meat thermometer, the center should read 145°F.) Remove and season with salt and pepper to taste. If cooking in two batches, rinse and wipe out the pan between batches, add the remaining chops, and cook as described for the first batch.

PORK CHOPS WITH CARAMELIZED BANANAS AND HERB AIOLI

4

NOTES / INGREDIENTS / METHOD:

Bananas in savory dishes are a welcome change of pace—the sweetness and natural creaminess are a great foil for meats. You'll also see them in the Thai Chicken Salad (page 70). The herb aioli ties this dish together: spread any leftover on sandwiches the next day.

HERB AIOLI
2 teaspoons chopped fresh rosemary leaves
2 teaspoons chopped fresh sage leaves
2 teaspoons chopped fresh thyme leaves
¼ cup parsley leaves
2 egg whites
½ teaspoon Dijon mustard
1 teaspoon lemon juice
¾ cup grapeseed or canola oil
Kosher salt

CARAMELIZED ONION AND BANANAS
Grapeseed or canola oil
1 sweet onion (such as Vidalia), peeled and sliced in circles ¼ inch thick
Kosher salt
2 slightly underripe bananas, peeled and cut into ½-inch pieces on the bias
3 tablespoons butter
4 rosemary sprigs
4 sage sprigs
6 thyme sprigs
2 garlic cloves, smashed
Cracked black peppercorns

4 Seared Brined Pork Chops (page 151)

Prepare the herb aioli In a blender, combine the chopped rosemary, sage, thyme, and parsley along with the egg whites, mustard, and lemon juice; blend until smooth. With the blender still running, slowly drizzle in the oil until the mixture emulsifies into a thick sauce. Season to taste with salt and thin with a little water, if desired.

Make the onion and bananas Heat a large sauté pan over medium-high heat with a slick of grapeseed oil. Once the oil shimmers, add the onion slices and season with salt. Cook over high heat until they char at the edges. Flip and brown the other sides, then remove the onion to a paper towel.

Lower the heat to medium and add some more oil, if necessary, to slick the bottom of the pan. Add the bananas and sauté until they caramelize. Remove from the pan and set aside.

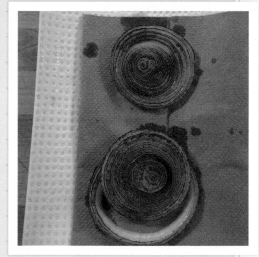

BROWN THE
ONION EDGES

Drop the butter into the pan along with the rosemary, sage, and thyme sprigs and the garlic, and cook to infuse the butter with herb flavor. When the butter is slightly browned, remove the pan from the heat.

Plate the pork chops with the caramelized onion and bananas. Drizzle with the browned butter and herbs, and dot with the herb aioli. Season with additional salt and the cracked peppercorns.

ALL THE FLAVORS IN THIS DISH BALANCE OUT

THIS IS A PERFECT
WEEKNIGHT
DINNER

PORK CHOPS WITH CREAMED KALE AND FENNEL-APRICOT SALAD

NOTES / INGREDIENTS / METHOD:

The Double-Creamed Spinach (page 232) was the inspiration for this creamed kale. We loved the technique of pureeing the greens, making for both great flavor and terrific presentation. Apricots and mustard balance out the dish, bringing forth the fruit and spice you want with pork.

CREAMED KALE
2 white onions
3 tablespoons olive oil
2 tablespoons butter
2 bunches of kale (about 1 to 1½ pounds; try to use two different varieties, like dinosaur and red)
Kosher salt
Freshly ground black pepper
1 cup heavy cream

2 tablespoons honey

FENNEL-APRICOT SALAD
1 fennel bulb
¼ cup whole-grain mustard
⅓ cup apricot jam
1 tablespoon extra-virgin olive oil

4 Seared Brined Pork Chops (page 151)

DICE THE ONIONS

Make the creamed kale Dice the onions. Heat 2 tablespoons of the olive oil and the butter in a Dutch oven or large saucepan over medium heat. Add the onions, and as the onions sweat, rip the kale from the stems, discard the stems, and roughly chop the leafy parts.

When the onions are translucent, season with salt. Add the kale and sweat until wilted. Season with more salt and some black pepper. Add the cream and honey, and cook the kale down until it is tender; this might be 15 minutes or as many as 40 minutes, depending on the tenderness of the kale. If the pot looks dry and the kale isn't fully cooked, add a little water; the kale should be saucy, not soupy.

Transfer half the kale to a blender and puree until smooth. Fold the puree back into the rest of the kale, season to taste with salt and pepper, and serve.

Make the fennel-apricot salad Thinly slice the fennel on a mandoline and place in a bowl of cold water in the fridge. Mix the mustard, jam, and olive oil in a small bowl. Toss the shaved fennel in the apricot mustard, and season to taste with salt.

WE USED BOTH DINOSAUR AND RED KALE FOR THIS

To serve, divide the kale onto 4 serving dishes, then top each with a pork chop and some fennel-apricot salad.

PORK CHOPS WITH SEARED SUMMER SQUASH, TOMATO, AND BLACK OLIVE TAPENADE

4

NOTES / INGREDIENTS / METHOD:

During the warm months, summer squash seems to be endless. This dish and the Spaghetti with Summer Squash and Pine Nuts (page 142) are two great ways to use it. The Provençal flavors of tomato, olives, and squash are perfect together. Use any extra tapenade on sandwiches or serve with a cheese plate.

3 summer squash: zucchini, pattypan squash, or whatever looks good at the farmers' market
2 large heirloom tomatoes
1 cup pitted Kalamata olives
2 garlic cloves
⅓ cup parsley leaves

Zest of 1 lemon
1 dried red chile
Extra-virgin olive oil
Kosher salt
Freshly ground black pepper
4 Seared Brined Pork Chops (page 151)
Marjoram leaves, for garnish

Slice the squash into rounds, and cut the tomatoes into quarters.

Add the olives to a food processor along with the garlic, parsley, lemon zest, and chile. Process until the tapenade forms a thick paste, adding olive oil as desired to achieve a smooth consistency.

Set a large sauté pan over medium-high heat and add enough olive oil to generously coat the bottom. When the oil shimmers, add the squash and tomatoes and season well with salt and pepper. Cook, undisturbed, until the bottoms of the vegetables are browning. Toss, then cook for 2 more minutes or just until cooked through.

Spread some of the tapenade on a serving dish. Place the vegetables on top of the tapenade, and then add the pork chops. Top with fresh marjoram and serve.

A MORTAR AND PESTLE WORK WELL HERE

080   PORK SCHNITZEL WITH SAGE AND CAPERS

4

NOTES / INGREDIENTS / METHOD:

Schnitzel can be any meat pounded thin, dipped in egg, coated with breadcrumbs, and sautéed lightly. I like it made with pork, but you can also easily make schnitzel with chicken. The sage and capers make this a classic.

A BIG SQUEEZE OF LEMON BRIGHTENS THIS UP

1 (2-pound) pork loin
Kosher salt
Freshly ground black pepper
2 cups all-purpose flour, plus more
2 cups panko breadcrumbs
8 thyme sprigs

1 bunch of fresh sage
4 eggs
2 tablespoons capers, rinsed
Grapeseed or vegetable oil, for frying
1 lemon, quartered

Slice the pork loin into 4 pieces about 1 inch thick. Place one by one into a large zippered plastic bag, but don't zip it shut. Using a mallet or a heavy skillet, gently but firmly pound the meat until it is ¼ inch thick. The slices will end up becoming quite large—almost covering a whole plate. Pound each slice, and season both sides with salt and pepper.

POUND THE MEAT ¼ INCH THICK

Add 2 cups flour to a large flat-bottomed vessel, such as a pie pan, for breading the pork. Pour the panko into a second flat-bottomed vessel. The panko will provide the crunch, and the flour will fill in the spaces. Remove the thyme leaves from the stems and add to the flour mixture, and season generously with salt and black pepper. Finely chop half of the sage leaves and add to the flour as well.

Lightly beat the eggs in a large bowl. Working with one slice at a time, dust the pork with the flour mixture, then dip in the egg. Allow excess egg to drip off, then coat in the breadcrumbs.

COAT THE PORK IN BREADCRUMBS FOR CRUNCH

Pour ¼ inch of oil into a large sauté pan and set it over medium heat. Once the oil is shimmering, add the remaining sage leaves and the capers, and fry until the sage is crisp. This will perfume the oil and create a garnish for the dish. Using a slotted spoon, remove the sage and capers to a paper towel.

Add a pork schnitzel to the pan by dipping the bottom of the schnitzel into the side of the pan closest to you, and then calmly lowering the rest of the slice away from you—this avoids any risk of splashing hot oil onto yourself. Once the schnitzel is browned on the edges, flip it gently with tongs and cook until a rich brown on the other side, 3 to 4 minutes per side. Drain on paper towels and keep warm in a 200°F oven until all the pork is cooked. Repeat with the remaining slices.

Season the schnitzel with salt. Place a slice on each plate, squeeze a little lemon juice over each, and top with fried sage and capers.

081 PORK CHOPS WITH ROASTED APPLE, BRUSSELS SPROUTS, AND BACON

4

NOTES / INGREDIENTS / METHOD:

THIS IS A GREAT FALL DINNER

Apples and pork chops are a classic marriage, and so are pork and cabbage. (Brussels sprouts are cousins of cabbage, after all.) So we glazed Brussels sprouts with apple cider to serve alongside these pork chops. The goat cheese gets soft from the residual heat of the pork and vegetables, melting into the dish and adding a nice, tangy contrast.

2 pounds Brussels sprouts
⅓ cup walnuts
6 slices bacon
2 apples, preferably Honeycrisp or Pink Lady
3 tablespoons extra-virgin olive oil
Kosher salt

Freshly ground black pepper
1 tablespoon butter
6 fresh sage leaves
1½ cups apple cider
4 Seared Brined Pork Chops (page 151)
4 ounces goat cheese, crumbled

Preheat the oven to 400°F. You want the Brussels sprouts in a variety of shapes and sizes: remove some leaves, cut some in half, and leave some smaller ones whole. Spread the sprout pieces on a sheet pan and sprinkle on the walnuts. Slice the bacon into ½-inch strips and add as well. Cut the apples into thin slices and add them also. Drizzle 2 tablespoons of the olive oil over all the ingredients, and season well with salt and pepper. Place in the oven.

Add the butter and remaining 1 tablespoon olive oil to a large sauté pan set over medium heat. Add the sage leaves and sauté until crisp, then drain on a paper towel. Add the apple cider and a few pinches of salt to the pan, and reduce to a glaze.

When the vegetables in the oven are golden brown, in 15 to 20 minutes, transfer them along with any drippings to the saucepan and toss in the glaze.

Place the vegetables on a serving dish, and top with the pork chops. Sprinkle on the goat cheese crumbles and the fried sage leaves, and serve.

PORK— LARGER CUTS

Larger cuts of meat typically require larger chunks of time to cook, but the recipes in this section have big payoffs. We used the brining idea from the "Pork Chops" chapter and the crispy skin technique from the Super-Crisp Roast Chicken (page 69) to take ham to the next level. But why stop at a well-roasted ham? We stuffed, rolled, and slow-roasted or smoked hams for additional flavor feasts. With these recipes, while the meat is roasting in the oven or smoking along in the Big Green Egg, there's a great chance to spend some time with your family or to get started on the side dishes. So, these special weekend meals are worth the effort. They're dishes that you will want to eat over and over again—and they make a ton of food, meaning guaranteed leftovers for the days to come.

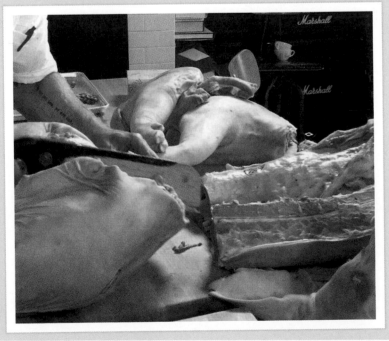

RECIPES:

- SLOW-ROASTED HAM "PORCHETTA" 163

- CARAMELIZED APPLE MUSTARD 166

- TURNIP PUREE 167

- HOUSE-SMOKED BACON 168

- SMOKE-ROASTED HAWAIIAN HAM 171

- SHRIMP AND SPAM LO MEIN 173

SLOW-ROASTED HAM "PORCHETTA"

NOTES / INGREDIENTS / METHOD:

This is really a ham cooked in the style of that great Italian roast, *porchetta*. For both this recipe and the Smoke-Roasted Hawaiian Ham (page 171), we made a flavorful puree, spread it on the meat, and rolled and tied it up before roasting. But another key here was to first inject the meat with a marinade—a fast way to impart flavor without having to marinate overnight. This porchetta-style ham is great with the Caramelized Apple Mustard and Turnip Puree that follow.

RECIPE CONTINUES

2 large white onions
1½ fennel bulbs
8 garlic cloves
2 Calabrian chiles or hot Italian
   peppers in oil
1 lemon
Extra-virgin olive oil
2 bay leaves

4 thyme sprigs
½ bunch of mustard greens,
   roughly chopped
1 cup golden raisins
Kosher salt
1 boneless skin-on ham,
   15 to 20 pounds, butterflied
Freshly ground black pepper

THE FENNEL
WILL BECOME A
FLAVORFUL PB
PUREE FOR THE
PORK

Preheat the oven to 250°F. Cut the onions and fennel in half, and then slice thin. Finely chop 5 garlic cloves and thinly slice the chiles. Using a vegetable peeler, take off three long, 1-inch-wide strips of peel from the lemon, and mince one of the strips.

Coat the bottom of a large sauté pan with olive oil and set over medium-high heat. When the oil is hot, add the onions, fennel, chopped garlic, chiles, bay leaves, and thyme. Allow the onions to sweat for about 5 minutes, until translucent, then add the mustard greens, raisins, 1 tablespoon salt, and the minced lemon peel. Cook, stirring, until the greens are wilted and tender, about 5 minutes more. Transfer the mixture to a food processor and puree to a paste.

Pour 1 cup of water into a saucepan; smash and add the remaining 3 garlic cloves, the 2 remaining strips of lemon peel, and 2 tablespoons salt. Bring the liquid to a boil, then remove from the heat and let cool to lukewarm.

With a sharp knife, score the skin of the ham in a crosshatch pattern, leaving 1-inch gaps between the scores. Flip the ham so that it's lying skin side down. Using a syringe or flavor injector, inject the steeped garlic-lemon liquid into the meat at regular intervals. Season the ham liberally with salt and pepper. Spread the meat with the mustard green puree. Roll the meat lengthwise into a log starting from the shorter end. Tie the meat together at 2-inch intervals using butcher's twine. As you roll, some of the puree will come out of the ham. Smear the fallen puree on any exposed flesh, but leave the skin uncovered.

Place the ham on a rack in the oven. Set a larger pan underneath it to catch any drippings, and roast for 5 to 6 hours, or until the skin is crisp and a thermometer inserted in the thickest part of the meat reads 150°F. Remove the ham from the oven and increase the heat to 450°F. Put the ham back in the oven and roast about 10 more minutes; the skin will puff up like pork cracklings. Remove from the oven. Let the meat rest for 20 minutes or more. Remove the twine. Cut the meat into ½-inch slices, and serve.

SMEAR THE PUREE
OVER THE PORK

ROLL UP THE HAM
LENGTHWISE

TIE THE ROLLED HAM
AT 2-INCH INTERVALS

THE HAM WILL LOOK
GREAT WHEN SLICED

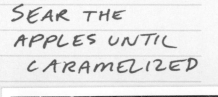

SEAR THE
APPLES UNTIL
CARAMELIZED

CARAMELIZED APPLE MUSTARD

Makes about 3 cups

Apples and mustard are both complements to pork on their own, so we combined them to make a condiment that is doubly delicious with the porchetta.

Grapeseed or vegetable oil
4 Pink Lady apples, cored and cut into eighths
2 cups unfiltered apple juice
1 cup apple cider vinegar
1 tablespoon Dijon mustard

1 tablespoon brown mustard seeds
1 tablespoon yellow mustard seeds
¼ cup chopped Medjool dates
Kosher salt
Marjoram leaves, for garnish

Coat the bottom of a large sauté pan or Dutch oven with some oil and set over medium-high heat. Add as many apples as will fit in the hot pan in one layer, and sear them until well caramelized. Flip them and caramelize the other side as well. If working in batches, remove the cooked apples and add any remaining, caramelizing as before.

When all of the apples are caramelized, combine them in the pan and add the apple juice, vinegar, mustard, both mustard seeds, dates, and a pinch of salt. Stir, bring to a boil, and turn down to a vigorous simmer, stirring occasionally. When the liquid reduces to a glaze, season to taste with salt. Transfer to a serving bowl and top with fresh marjoram leaves.

So DELICIOUS
WITH PORK →

TURNIP PUREE

Serves 6 to 8

Turnips are an underrated root vegetable, in my opinion. This puree uses their sweet, earthy flavor for a side dish that is rich without being too heavy. It's the perfect match for the pork. We topped the puree with roasted turnips for a nice texture contrast, showcasing another easy way to prepare the vegetable. Save the turnip greens for another use—they are packed with nutrients and are a common side dish in the South.

CUT INTO LARGE DICE

1 large white onion
6 tablespoons butter
2 tablespoons grapeseed or
    vegetable oil
Kosher salt
4 large turnips (about 2½ pounds)

4 cups whole milk
1 bay leaf
1 thyme sprig
Extra-virgin olive oil
Flaky sea salt
Freshly ground black pepper

Finely dice the onion. Place 2 tablespoons of the butter and the oil in a large saucepan over medium heat. When the butter is melted, add the onion and 1 teaspoon salt. Sweat the onion until translucent; you do not want to color it.

INFUSE WITH BAY LEAF AND THYME

Peel the turnips, and cut one half of 1 turnip into 4 wedges, and set aside. Cut the remaining turnips into large dice. Add the diced turnips, a pinch of salt, the milk, bay leaf, and thyme to the saucepan. Bring to a boil, then reduce to a simmer and cook about 20 minutes, until you can pierce the turnips easily with a fork. Let cool for a few minutes.

Meanwhile, slick a sauté pan with some olive oil and set over high heat. When the oil shimmers, add the remaining turnip wedges and sear until caramelized on both sides. Sprinkle lightly with salt.

Remove and discard the thyme sprig and bay leaf from the cooked turnips. Drain, reserving the milk, and transfer to a blender. Add half the milk and the remaining 4 tablespoons butter. Blend until smoothed to the consistency of rich mashed potatoes. If the puree is very thick, blend in a little more of the milk; if it's too thin, transfer back to the saucepan and simmer to reduce the liquid and tighten it up. Taste for seasoning, and add salt as necessary.

Transfer the puree to a serving dish. Garnish with the caramelized turnip wedges, a drizzle of olive oil, and a sprinkle of the flaky sea salt and black pepper.

HOUSE-SMOKED BACON

✷ NOTE: PINK SALT, ALSO KNOWN AS CURE #1, TINTED CURING MIX, OR DQ CURE, IS USED TO PREVENT UNWANTED BACTERIAL GROWTH, AND IT ALSO GIVES THE MEAT A DISTINCT "CURED" FLAVOR. IT'S EASILY AVAILABLE ONLINE OR IN MANY BUTCHER SHOPS.

NOTES / INGREDIENTS / METHOD:

Making your own bacon is a pretty cool experience, since you can control the quality of pork, the seasoning, and the kind of smoke. After we cured our bacon for a few days in an herb seasoning, we smoked it for 3 hours. We loved using our Big Green Egg for the smoking, but use any other smoker you like. Whatever you use, the results are so worth the effort. Just consider how it will take your BLTs to a whole new level.

5 thyme sprigs
4 bay leaves
¼ cup kosher salt
2 teaspoons pink salt (see Note) ✷
4 tablespoons freshly ground
   black pepper
¼ cup dark brown sugar

1 (5-pound) slab of pork belly
   (with or without skin)

Special equipment: a smoker
   that will accommodate the
   pork, wood chips (hickory or
   applewood recommended)

Finely crush the thyme sprigs and bay leaves using a mortar and pestle or a food processor, or mince with a knife. Combine with the salts, pepper, and brown sugar in a small bowl.

Rub the seasoning onto both sides of the pork belly. Place the seasoned belly in a large zippered plastic bag, close the bag, and set it in the refrigerator to cure for 5 days. The pork will leach some liquid; flip the bag daily so that the brine has even contact with the meat.

Set your smoker to 225°F. Remove the pork from the bag and discard the liquid. Rinse the meat and pat dry. Place in the smoker and smoke for 3 hours, or until it has a nice tan from the smoke, a nice firm feel, and an internal temperature of 150°F.

IF YOU LOVE BACON, TRY MAKING YOUR OWN

Place the smoked bacon on a sheet pan. If your bacon includes the skin, you can slice the skin off and keep it as a flavoring for stews and such. Place another pan on top of the bacon and set a heavy object on top, such as a cast-iron pan. When the bacon has cooled to room temperature, chill it overnight, pressed, in the fridge.

Slice and cook the bacon as desired, keeping the rest tightly wrapped in plastic wrap.

THE SMELL OF BACON IS THE BEST SMELL TO WAKE UP TO

AN AWESOME MEAL FOR A BIG PARTY

SMOKE-ROASTED HAWAIIAN HAM

30 to 40   **086–087**

NOTES / INGREDIENTS / METHOD:

After we developed the Slow-Roasted Ham "Porchetta" (page 163), we thought it would be great to use a similar method to put a spin on Hawaiian ham, inspired by both Asian and Polynesian influences. We used the same method to inject the meat, spread it with a puree, and roll and tie it, but then we smoked the ham to add even more flavor. You'll use half a fresh pineapple and half a can of Spam in this recipe—after all, Hawaiians eat more Spam than anyone else in America, and why not flavor the meat with more meat?—so save the other halves for Shrimp and Spam Lo Mein (page 173), which is a lot of fun as an accompanying dish. You will likely have a lot of leftovers. The ham is great the next day in sandwiches.

1 white onion
1 serrano chile
A 2-inch piece of fresh ginger
6 garlic cloves
Grapeseed or vegetable oil
1 fresh pineapple
1 can of Spam
1 bunch of green onions
4 thyme sprigs
1 bay leaf

1½ cups soy sauce
1 tablespoon toasted sesame oil
1 boneless ham, 15 to 20 pounds, skin removed, butterflied
Shrimp and Spam Lo Mein (recipe follows)

Special equipment: flavor injector, a smoker that accommodates the pork (we used a large Big Green Egg), wood chips

Set your smoker to 250°F, using your favorite wood chips.

Cut the onion in half and then into thin slices. Thinly slice the chile. Using a spoon, scrape the skin off of the ginger, and chop the ginger very fine. Finely chop the garlic.

Slick the bottom of a large saucepan with some oil and place over high heat. When the oil is shimmering, add the onion, chile, ginger, and garlic to the pan and cook, stirring, until very aromatic. Turn the heat down to medium and continue cooking until the onion is nicely browned.

Remove the top and bottom of the pineapple. Stand the pineapple up, cut off the skin, and cut the flesh from the core. Finely dice half of the pineapple and reserve the remainder for the lo mein. Dice half the Spam and reserve the remainder for another use. Chop the green onions, keeping the green and white parts separate.

RECIPE CONTINUES

Add the pineapple, Spam, the thyme, and bay leaf to the pan. Add ½ cup of the soy sauce and the sesame oil, and cook for about 5 more minutes. Transfer the mixture to a food processor and puree. Fold in most of the green onion tops, reserving a small amount of the tops and all of the whites for a garnish.

Lay the ham on your work surface. Using a syringe or a flavor injector, inject the remaining 1 cup soy sauce into the ham. Spread the meat with the puree. Roll up the ham lengthwise, starting from the shorter end. Tie the log at 3-inch intervals using butcher's twine. As you roll, some of the puree will come out of the ham; smear the fallen puree on the outside of the roll. (See photographs on page 165.)

Place the ham in the smoker and smoke for 5 to 6 hours, or until a thermometer inserted in the thickest part of the meat reads 150°F. When finished, remove from the smoker and let cool to handle. Remove the butcher's twine and slice. Garnish with the reserved green onion tops and whites. Serve, with the lo mein if desired.

WE USED THE
BIG GREEN EGG
TO SMOKE THIS
HAM (AND THE
BACON, TOO)

SHRIMP AND SPAM LO MEIN

Serves 4

This lo mein, a mix of Asian and Island flavors, is the perfect dish to serve alongside the Smoke-Roasted Hawaiian Ham. Since we already had the Spam, we decided to explore what it had to offer and came up with this surf-and-turf noodle dish that would also be fantastic on its own.

1 (8-ounce) package dried lo mein noodles (thick Chinese wheat noodles)

3 tablespoons peanut oil, plus more as needed

A ½-inch piece of fresh ginger

3 garlic cloves

1 bunch of green onions

1 carrot

1 serrano chile

½ can of Spam

1 pound shrimp, shelled

1 cup chicken stock

2 tablespoons cornstarch

¼ cup soy sauce

1 tablespoon toasted sesame oil

1 tablespoon rice vinegar

1 cup diced fresh pineapple

Kosher salt

Freshly ground black pepper

RECIPE CONTINUES

THESE NOODLES ARE ALSO GREAT COLD, RIGHT OUT OF THE FRIDGE

Cook the noodles in a large pot of boiling water for 3 minutes, until just tender. Drain well and toss with 3 tablespoons of the peanut oil.

Using a spoon, scrape the skin off the ginger and mince the ginger. Mince the garlic. Finely chop the green onion whites and greens, keeping them separate. Cut the carrot into matchsticks. Slice the chile into thin rings. Dice the Spam. If the shrimp are large, cut them in half.

In a measuring cup, combine the chicken stock, cornstarch, soy sauce, sesame oil, and vinegar; whisk until there are no lumps.

Coat a large sauté pan with some peanut oil and set over high heat. When the oil is hot but not quite smoking, add the ginger, garlic, and chile and cook, stirring, until aromatic—it will smell fantastic. Add the carrot, green onion whites, and pineapple, and cook for 2 minutes more, until the carrot is starting to soften but still has bite. Season with salt and move the vegetables to a large bowl.

Add the shrimp to the pan with a generous pinch of salt and add the Spam. Cook until the shrimp are just done. Transfer to the bowl.

Add some more peanut oil, if necessary, to keep the pan coated, then add the noodles to the pan, and allow them to get some crunch on the edges. Then add the noodles to the bowl.

Give the cornstarch mixture a quick stir and add to the pan, cooking it down until it thickens into a sauce. Turn off the heat.

Toss all the ingredients in the bowl, then drizzle the sauce over, to taste.

Toss the green onion tops into the bowl with the noodles. Season to taste with salt and freshly ground black pepper.

IF DESIRED, RESERVE SOME SAUCE TO DRIZZLE OVER THE HAM AS WELL.

PORK CARNITAS TACOS

Living in California, I'm lucky to have tons of flavorful Mexican food around me all the time. Our neighbors to the south know how to cook in a balanced way—there is always a squeeze of lime or a hint of chile in each bite. For my wife's birthday last year, we went to Cabo San Lucas for a few days with some friends, and one night we had dinner at a farm in the foothills of the mountains. We were all blown away by the amazing food that's happening in Mexico, and it's exciting to try to replicate those flavors up here. As we had all that fresh pork in the Test Kitchen, we thought of more ways to use it. And since tacos were on our recipe-development list, we figured it would be great to bring them together.

One of my favorite things about tacos is the endless array of condiments they come with. In California, we have delicious avocados on pretty much a year-round basis, so guacamole is a no-brainer. But making salsa at home can be so much more than just chopping ripe tomatoes and onions: by char-roasting vegetables or using different types of tomatoes, you can come up with some unique condiments that make entertaining even more fun.

RECIPES:

- PORK CARNITAS TACOS WITH
  TOMATILLO SALSA VERDE   177

- GUACAMOLE   180

- FRESH TORTILLA CHIPS AND
  ROASTED TOMATO - PEPPER SALSA   182

- ROASTED AND GRILLED
  MEXICAN CORN   184

- HIBISCUS ESCABECHE   186

PORK CARNITAS TACOS WITH TOMATILLO SALSA VERDE

NOTES / INGREDIENTS / METHOD:

Tacos are an ideal dinner party dish—guests add the toppings they want—and slow-braised and crisped pork carnitas are one of our favorite taco fillings. Traditionally fried in lard, these carnitas are more healthfully braised in tomatillo salsa, which gives the pork a kick as well. The condiments that follow make this taco party really special.

CARNITAS
1 (2-pound) Boston butt or boneless pork shoulder
Kosher salt
Freshly ground black pepper
Grapeseed or vegetable oil
3 garlic cloves
1 carrot
½ onion
½ jalapeño pepper
1 teaspoon ground cumin
1 teaspoon ground coriander
2 bay leaves
1 marjoram sprig
1 thyme sprig

½ cup Tomatillo Salsa Verde (recipe follows)

FOR SERVING
Corn tortillas
Tomatillo Salsa Verde (recipe follows)
Roasted Tomato–Pepper Salsa (page 182)
Guacamole (page 180)
Hibiscus Escabeche (page 186)
Cotija cheese, crumbled
Lime wedges
Sliced radishes

Preheat the oven to 350°F.

Make the carnitas Cut the pork into 1-inch cubes. Season the meat with salt and pepper.

Heat a large Dutch oven or deep, oven-safe sauté pan over medium-high heat. Coat the pan with some oil; when the oil is shimmering, add as many pork cubes as will fit comfortably in one layer and sear. When the pork is richly browned on one side, flip the pieces with tongs to brown the other side. Remove the first batch of pork to a bowl, deglaze the pan with a little bit of water to pick up the browned bits, and add that to the bowl. Wipe out the pan, coat with a bit more of the oil, and reheat; then add the next batch of meat. Repeat as necessary, always reheating the pan before adding the next batch of pork cubes.

While the meat browns, cut the garlic, carrot, onion, and jalapeño into large chunks.

CUT THE PORK INTO 1-INCH CUBES

RECIPE CONTINUES

Return all the pork to the pan and add the vegetables, the cumin, coriander, bay leaves, marjoram, and thyme. Stir well, then add the tomatillo salsa. Bring the salsa to a boil, turn off the heat, and cover the pan with a tight-fitting lid. Place the pan in the oven and cook for 1½ to 2 hours, until the meat is very tender and falls apart. Check on the meat after the first 30 minutes; if it looks dry, add a little bit of water, re-cover, and continue cooking, checking to see if you need more liquid every 30 minutes or so.

Preheat the oven to broil. Uncover the pan and broil 5 to 10 minutes, until the meat gets crisp on top. Add a little water if necessary, so that there is some liquid covering the bottom of the pan.

With a spoon, break the meat up in the pan and remove the carrot. Transfer the pork to a serving dish and keep warm.

Get ready to serve Lay some of the tortillas on a sheet pan and place under the broiling element for a few seconds, just until they are hot. Stack them and wrap in a slightly moist towel to keep warm as you heat more tortillas.

Place the salsas, guacamole, escabeche, cotija, lime, and radishes in separate dishes. Place the warmed tortillas nearby. Have guests assemble the tacos as desired.

TOMATILLO SALSA VERDE

Makes about 4 cups

10 tomatillos
½ poblano pepper
½ jalapeño pepper
½ onion
2 garlic cloves
⅓ cup chopped cilantro

½ teaspoon cumin seeds
½ teaspoon ground coriander
¼ cup agave nectar or honey
¼ cup extra-virgin olive oil
Juice of 2 limes
Kosher salt

Remove the paper husks from the tomatillos and rinse the tomatillos in cool water to remove any sticky residue. Roughly chop the tomatillos with the poblano, jalapeño, onion, and garlic. Add along with the cilantro, cumin, coriander, and agave nectar to a food processor and puree. Drizzle in the olive oil through the opening with the processor running. Squeeze in the lime juice and season to taste with salt. Transfer to a bowl for serving.

THE PORK AND VEGETABLES WILL
BUILD BIG FLAVORS DURING THE
COOKING PROCESS

GUACAMOLE

MAKES ABOUT 4 CUPS, DEPENDING ON THE AVOCADOS

I LIKE MY GUACAMOLE SIMPLE — ONLY THE ESSENTIALS

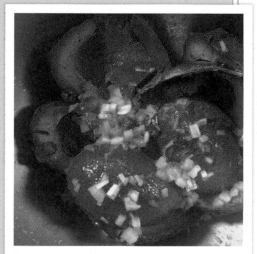

NOTES / INGREDIENTS / METHOD:

Latin American flavors, especially Mexican, are very important to cuisine in the United States, particularly in California. Our guacamole has a clean flavor that highlights the avocado. I use serranos over jalapeños in this recipe; the heat's a little more aggressive, but I love the grassy and citrus flavors of serranos.

5 ripe Hass avocados
Juice of 2 limes
½ small white onion, finely chopped
1 serrano chile, or more as desired

½ bunch of cilantro, leaves finely chopped
Kosher salt
Freshly ground black pepper
Extra-virgin olive oil
1 radish, thinly shaved

Slice the avocados all the way around from top to bottom, and twist the halves to separate them. Carefully tap the pit with a sharp knife, twist, and it will come right out. Scoop the avocado flesh into a large bowl. Add some of the lime juice as you prepare the avocados to prevent the flesh from browning.

Add the onion to the bowl. Carefully slice open the chile lengthwise and cut out and discard the seeds and ribs (these are the hottest part; if you love heat, feel free to include them). Finely slice the chile and add to the bowl. Use a fork to mash the mixture, leaving some chunks of avocado for texture.

Add as much of the cilantro and the remaining lime juice as you like, and season with salt and pepper. Finish with a drizzle of olive oil and garnish with the radish shavings (and more chile slices, if desired). Transfer to a bowl for serving.

RADISHES BRING A POP
OF FLAVOR (AND COLOR)

FRESH TORTILLA CHIPS AND ROASTED TOMATO–PEPPER SALSA

6

NOTES / INGREDIENTS / METHOD:

Making your own tortilla chips is not as hard as it might sound, and they are guaranteed to be devoured faster than the ones you get from the store. Fresh-from-the-fryer chips are impossible to resist, and are the perfect scooping device for guacamole and salsa.

12 corn tortillas (look for packages with "masa harina" in the ingredients)

Grapeseed or canola oil, for frying
Kosher salt

Cut the tortillas into 4 wedges. Heat 3 inches of oil to 360°F in a large pot over medium-high heat. While the oil is heating, set a clean towel or paper towels on a sheet tray for draining.

Add the tortillas to the oil a handful at a time, leaving enough room for them to swim around a bit. Agitate the tortillas with a long metal spoon so they don't stick together. Once they are golden brown, remove the chips with a spider or slotted spoon to the towel to drain, and season with salt while still hot.

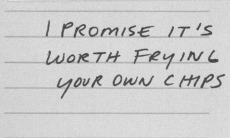

I PROMISE IT'S WORTH FRYING YOUR OWN CHIPS

ROASTED TOMATO–PEPPER SALSA

Makes about 6 cups

Roasting the vegetables in this salsa concentrates the flavors by reducing the water content while adding a charbroiled taste.

4 ripe tomatoes
2 poblano peppers
1 serrano chile
½ onion
2 garlic cloves
3 tablespoons extra-virgin olive oil

1 teaspoon cumin seeds
Kosher salt
⅓ cup cilantro leaves

Preheat the oven to broil. Cut an X into the tops of the tomatoes, near the stem, leaving the stems on, and place them on a sheet tray. Slice the poblanos and serrano in half lengthwise, slice the onion into rings, and lightly crush the garlic. Spread the vegetables on a sheet tray. Drizzle with 1 tablespoon of olive oil, the cumin seeds, and 1 teaspoon salt. Lightly toss and broil for approximately 15 minutes, or until the vegetables are soft and have some dark char.

Let the vegetables cool down a bit, then remove some of the charred tomato skin. Transfer the vegetables to a food processor, and add any juices from the pan. Pulse the vegetables just to chop them a bit. Add the remaining 2 tablespoons oil, 1 teaspoon salt, and the cilantro, and pulse again until you reach a chunky salsa texture. Stir in more salt to taste.

THIS SPREAD IS IRRESISTIBLE

ROASTED AND GRILLED MEXICAN CORN

6

NOTES / INGREDIENTS / METHOD:

A major topic of conversation in the Test Kitchen centers on how to maximize flavor. So many corn recipes have you throw the husked cobs in boiling water, but all that does is extract the corn flavor and put it into water that ultimately gets thrown away. So, instead of boiling corn before putting it on the grill, we roasted it while it was in the husk, concentrating the corn flavor instead of getting rid of it. Inspired by the Mexican street snack called *elotes,* we add acid, fat, and spice to the grilled corn, building a balanced and refreshing side dish.

6 ears of corn, with husks and silks
½ cup mayonnaise
½ cup cotija cheese (a salty Mexican cow's milk cheese; you can substitute feta or Parmesan)

Juice of 1 lime
Kosher salt
Pimentón (smoked paprika) or dark chili powder (optional)

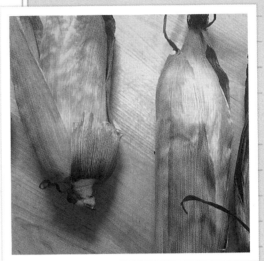

FIRST ROAST THE CORN

Preheat the oven to 375°F.

Without peeling back the husks or pulling off the silks, place the corn on a sheet pan and roast for 25 minutes. When done, the husks will look like parchment paper.

While the corn cooks, preheat the grill to high. (If you're using a grill pan, preheat it over medium-low heat, being careful not to get it smoking hot too soon.)

Pull back the husks but keep them on the cob, and remove the silks. Tie the husks in a knot to create a handle that is attached to the cob. (Or, you can stop here and eat the corn right now.) Place the corn directly on a very hot grill (or on a grill pan) to get a little charred flavor and texture. When the corn has grill marks on both sides, remove it.

Using a brush, slather mayonnaise on each cob, then crumble on the cheese and press it on with your hands to ensure it sticks. Squeeze the lime juice over the cobs, then sprinkle with salt and dust with the pimentón, if using. Serve immediately.

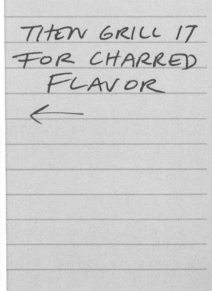

THEN GRILL IT FOR CHARRED FLAVOR
←

HIBISCUS ESCABECHE

MAKES ABOUT 6 CUPS

HIBISCUS TURNS THE PICKLES AN INTENSE MAGENTA

NOTES / INGREDIENTS / METHOD:

We're lucky to have a ton of authentic Mexican restaurants in California, where you'll find pickled carrots, onions, and peppers—called *escabeche*—on the tables. The spicy, tart kick of these condiments is a great complement for all kinds of tacos. We put a Test Kitchen spin on ours by adding dried hibiscus flowers to the brine, which adds a floral, fruit flavor and turns the pickles a stunning magenta. (They look fantastic in a glass jar in your fridge even after the tacos are gone.)

1 cup white vinegar
1 cup sugar
2 tablespoons salt
4 carrots
2 jalapeño peppers
2 mild red chiles, such as Jimmy Nardellos
1 white onion
½ teaspoon ground coriander
½ teaspoon black pepper

¼ teaspoon fennel seeds
½ teaspoon ground cumin
½ teaspoon yellow mustard seeds
½ teaspoon brown mustard seeds
¼ cup dried hibiscus flowers (also called *jamaica*), lightly crushed
2 bay leaves
1 thyme sprig
1 pound ice cubes

Whisk together the vinegar, sugar, and salt in a large mixing bowl. Peel the carrots and slice into ¼-inch-thick coins. Also slice the jalapeños and mild chiles ¼ inch thick. Julienne the onion. Combine the vegetables in a bowl, and add the coriander, pepper, fennel seeds, cumin, both mustard seeds, hibiscus, bay leaves, and thyme. Stir to combine. Stir the ice into the bowl. Once the ice melts, the pickles will be ready.

Transfer the pickled vegetables to a serving dish or a jar. In an airtight container, they will last for two weeks in the refrigerator.

POTATOES

How can mashed potatoes or french fries be made more exciting? We took a true Test Kitchen approach to some of our favorite foods, thinking about why we love them—whether it's for their texture, flavor, emotion-evoking powers, or all of the above.

A big plate of hot, crispy french fries is irresistible (go ahead; see if you can manage not to sneak one off the plate before they are served). So we came up with a way to make them crisper yet. Similarly, smooth mashed potatoes are the ultimate comfort food, and we amped up the natural potato flavor, so they wouldn't always have to play second fiddle.

These potato recipes were some of the first we tackled in the Test Kitchen, and our discoveries and innovations were motivation to continue down this path. While potatoes might not seem like the most exciting food category, when done right they are fantastic, whether paired with another dish or eaten on their own.

RECIPES:

- FRENCH FRIES WITH
  ROASTED GARLIC AIOLI   189

- EXTRA POTATO-Y
  MASHED POTATOES   192

- MARGE'S POTATO SALAD   194

- GARLIC-HERB POTATO CHIPS   197

FRENCH FRIES WITH ROASTED GARLIC AIOLI

NOTES / INGREDIENTS / METHOD:

The french fry can be the perfect food if done well—long, crisp, golden brown, salty, and satisfying. After many tests, these have been found to be the crispiest, fluffiest, most perfect french fries we've ever had. The key is the three-step cooking process. It's not the simplest method, but once you taste these fries, I think you'll agree you've never had better ones. As for the roasted garlic aioli, when is that ever *not* delicious?

RECIPE CONTINUES

3 large russet potatoes (these have the perfect starch content for fries)
4 tablespoons white vinegar
2 quarts grapeseed or canola oil

½ cup parsley leaves
Kosher salt
Flaky sea salt
Roasted Garlic Aioli (recipe follows)

Cut the potatoes into ¼-inch slices, then into ¼-inch sticks. Try to cut all the fries to the same size, so that they cook evenly. Bring a gallon of water to a boil over high heat in a pot, then add the vinegar. Pour in the potatoes, bring the water back up to a strong simmer, and simmer for 12 minutes. Gently drain the potatoes so you don't break them, and blot very dry on towels.

In a large pot with several inches of clearance, heat the oil to 390°F over medium-high heat. Carefully add all the potatoes, and fry for 1 minute to start building up the wall of the fry. Remove the fries to a towel-lined sheet tray and let cool to room temperature. Place the fries in the freezer for at least 2 hours, or even overnight.

Reheat the oil to 375°F. Add the frozen potatoes and fry for 3½ minutes, or until your desired color, from pale golden to brown. Ten seconds before the fries are done, add half of the parsley to the hot oil.

Transfer the fries and parsley to a towel-lined sheet tray and season with kosher salt. Finely chop the rest of the parsley and sprinkle over the fries. Finish with a sprinkling of flaky salt. Serve hot, with the aioli.

ROASTED GARLIC AIOLI

Makes about 2 cups

1 head of garlic, top ½ inch sliced off, exposing the tops of the cloves
Extra-virgin olive oil
Kosher salt

1 whole egg plus 2 yolks
2 teaspoons Dijon mustard
Juice of 1½ lemons
1 cup grapeseed or canola oil

Preheat the oven to 400°F. Place the garlic on a sheet of foil, drizzle with a little olive oil, sprinkle with salt, and close the foil around the garlic. Roast the garlic for 30 minutes, or until very soft.

Add the egg and yolks, mustard, and lemon juice to a blender and process to combine. Squeeze the roasted cloves out of their paper husks and into the blender, and blend again. With the machine running, slowly add the grapeseed oil to create a thick sauce. Add 2 tablespoons of water and blend again. If the mixture is too thick, add a bit more water. Add 1 tablespoon olive oil and salt to taste. (The aioli can keep for a week in the refrigerator in an airtight container.)

SIMMER POTATOES
IN WATER
AND VINEGAR

A TWO-PART
FRY MAKES THEM
SUPER-CRISPY

THE FRENCH DON'T FRY LIKE THIS

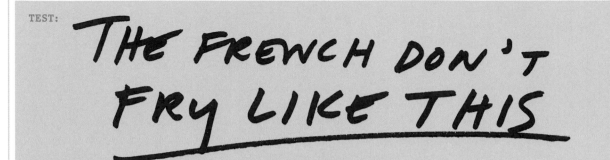

Traditional recipes for french fries have you cook the potatoes in two stages: first a low-temperature fry, then after a cool-down, another dip into oil, this time hotter, to crisp them up. But after subjecting many potatoes to this fate, we determined that a *three*-step process was key to getting the best french fries, with a detour into a freezer.

First, we simmered the potatoes in a light vinegar solution. The acid maintains the internal structure of the potato, while the heat causes the starches on the exterior of the potato to dissolve and glue together, forming a thick crust. Next, we quick-fried the potatoes to set that crust, and then we cooled and froze the potatoes. Freezing causes the water molecules to form jagged ice crystals within the potatoes, breaking open the cell walls and leading to more rapid evaporation during the final cooking process. Removing this moisture gives an extra-fluffy interior, and because there's less steam to make the fries soggy, it keeps them crisper. Finally, we fried the potatoes at a higher heat to finish them, adding herbs at the very end to perfume them and make a great garnish. We admit it's not the quickest way to make fries, but we think these are the most irresistible fries you'll ever have.

097

EXTRA POTATO-Y MASHED POTATOES

4 to 6

NOTES / INGREDIENTS / METHOD:

When making mashed potatoes, typically one cooks them in water, then pours that cooking water down the drain, which means all the potato flavor in the water is thrown away. So, we figured, why not cook the potatoes directly in the cream that would be added later on? We love the great potato flavor that results. Be sure, though, to start the potatoes in cold cream; if you add them to a hot liquid, the exterior starts to disintegrate before the inside has a chance to cook.

2 pounds Yukon Gold potatoes, peeled

2 cups heavy cream, cold

3 garlic cloves

½ cup (1 stick) unsalted butter, cut into chunks

Kosher salt

Extra-virgin olive oil

Coarse sea salt

Cut the potatoes into 2- to 3-inch chunks. Add them to a medium pot with the cream, garlic, butter, and salt to taste. Bring to a boil over medium-high heat, then turn down to a simmer and cook for about 25 minutes, until the potatoes are easily pierced with a fork.

Place a colander over a bowl. Pour the potatoes through the colander, reserving the hot cream in the bowl. Shake the potatoes to drain off the excess liquid. Scoop the potatoes into a ricer (or you could mash them with a fork for a chunkier texture). Rice the potatoes, occasionally clearing the sides of the ricer with a spoon. Pour the still-hot cream over the potatoes in small increments, folding in to combine, until you get your desired consistency. Season with olive oil and a sprinkle of sea salt, and serve immediately or keep warm.

DRAIN WELL,
THEN RECOMBINE

098

MARGE'S POTATO SALAD

4 to 6

NOTES / INGREDIENTS / METHOD:

This family standby is my mother-in-law's recipe. It has withstood the test of time because of its ideal balance of flavors and textures, and all the ingredients, from the hard-boiled eggs to the capers, bring something to the mix. I have tweaked it over time, though. We add a lot of herbs to keep the salad fresh and California-inspired, for example. And, for this latest version, I fell in love with dressing the potatoes while they're still warm, so they absorb the flavor. Use smaller Yukon Gold potatoes for a creamier texture and sweetness. And smaller potatoes can stay whole as you cook them, so you don't leach any potato flavor into the water.

**2 pounds small Yukon Gold
   potatoes**
¾ cup mayonnaise
¾ cup sour cream
1 tablespoon Dijon mustard
Juice of ½ lemon
1 teaspoon pickle juice
Kosher salt
1 dill pickle
1 red onion
½ cup parsley

⅓ cup dill
⅓ cup chives
2 green onions
2 tablespoons capers
Extra-virgin olive oil
Freshly ground black pepper
2 hard-boiled eggs, cut in half
**Herbs for garnish: mint, dill,
   parsley, chives**
Coarse sea salt

DRESSING WHILE WARM = MORE FLAVOR ABSORPTION

Put the potatoes into a big saucepan of cold salted water. Bring to a simmer over medium-high heat, and simmer for 15 to 20 minutes, until a paring knife poked into them goes in without resistance. Drain the potatoes in a colander and transfer onto a sheet tray to dry.

Stir together the mayonnaise, sour cream, mustard, lemon juice, pickle juice, and a pinch of salt in a bowl. Finely chop the dill pickle and add to the bowl.

Peel the outer layers of the red onion and dice (about ⅓ cup), and add the diced onion to the bowl. Thinly slice the center portion of the onion into rings and reserve for the garnish. Finely chop the parsley, dill, chives, green onions, and capers, and add to the dressing as well. Stir to combine, and season to taste with olive oil, salt, and pepper.

While the potatoes are still warm but cool enough to handle, lightly crush them between your fingers into a large mixing bowl. Pour the dressing over the potatoes and toss to coat well. Taste and adjust the seasoning with additional salt and pepper.

Transfer the potato salad to a serving dish. Garnish with the hard-boiled eggs and the red onion rings. Add the garnish herbs and finish with a drizzle of olive oil, a sprinkle of sea salt, and freshly ground black pepper.

GARLIC-HERB POTATO CHIPS

4 to 6

NOTES / INGREDIENTS / METHOD:

We keep bowls of potato chips on the bar at both Wayfare Tavern and El Paseo; they are a welcome snack that immediately makes guests feel at home. But these chips also happen to be impossible to stop eating, and here's why: We use Kennebec potatoes, which are firm and starchy. We rinse the potato slices before frying, removing excess starch and sugar, so the chips don't burn before they are fully cooked. And we infuse the cooking oil with garlic and herbs. Here, we give you two frying options: one yields chips with a delicate crispness, the other offers more crunch.

3 large russet or Kennebec potatoes
Grapeseed or canola oil, for frying
1 head of garlic
2 parsley sprigs

4 sage sprigs
3 rosemary sprigs
3 thyme sprigs
Kosher salt

Wash the potatoes, but don't peel them; the skin provides extra flavor and a rustic, homemade look. Using a mandoline, slice the potatoes, being sure to use the guard to protect your hands. If you like a crunchy kettle-style chip, slice the potatoes a bit thicker, ⅛ inch or so, and fry with the two-stage method below. If you prefer crisp, delicate chips, slice the potatoes very thin and use the single-stage method. Either way, slice the potatoes directly into a large bowl of cool water. Use firm, even pressure to get full circles of potatoes. The water will turn cloudy as the potato starch rinses off; that's good—otherwise the potatoes will caramelize too quickly in the hot oil and the chips will burn. Change the water in the bowl, agitating the slices with your hands, until the water is clear.

Heat 5 inches of oil in a tall, deep pot with a clip-on thermometer over medium-high heat to 350°F. Drain the potatoes and pat very dry with a clean towel (water and hot oil do not get along!).

Smash the garlic with the heel of your hand and remove the excess paper husks (but not all of them). Pull apart the cloves, and fry them whole, unpeeled, in the oil until browned and soft, about 2 minutes.

RINSE THE STARCH OFF THE POTATOES

RECIPE CONTINUES

Add the parsley, sage, rosemary sprigs, and thyme sprigs and fry until just crisp, another minute or two. Using a metal slotted spoon, transfer the fried herbs and garlic to a towel-lined plate.

For thin, delicate chips, bring the oil temperature up to 360°F. Add the potato slices quickly but carefully. Stir so that they remain separate. Maintain the heat at 350°F and fry until the chips are light and golden brown, 4 to 6 minutes. Transfer to a towel-lined sheet pan and season immediately with salt.

For thicker, crunchier chips, use the two-stage method. Let the oil cool to 260°F. Add the potatoes, and stir so that they separate. Maintain the heat at 250°F and fry for 8 to 10 minutes, until the potatoes are cooked, firm, but still pale. Transfer to a towel-lined sheet pan to drain. Increase the heat to raise the temperature to 350°F. Add the potatoes and fry again until golden brown, 2 to 3 minutes. Transfer to fresh towels on the sheet pan, and season with salt.

Toss the chips with the fried herbs, garlic, and more salt to taste.

CHOOSE THE COOKING METHOD BASED ON THE TEXTURE YOU WANT

RISOTTO

Risotto has been around for hundreds of years, and it seems that the technique we've all learned from the Northern Italians hasn't changed much in that time span. When we started thinking about risotto in the Test Kitchen, I asked Tolan if she ever makes it. She said that while she likes to, she doesn't feel like she can stand next to the stove, constantly stirring, for the thirty minutes it takes to get the rice cooked and creamy. Well, there was our challenge: find a way to make risotto without being chained to the stove. After first making a traditional risotto, we tried a no-stir method and it worked shockingly well. There was the creamy texture we all adore, but no one had to constantly ladle in warm broth and stir.

Risotto has two qualities I love: it is easily multiplied to feed a crowd, and it is a blank canvas for whatever is in season or in the back of your pantry. You could easily have a different risotto on the table each week. Keep a bag of Arborio rice in your pantry, and you can always whip up a batch if you are pressed for time to get dinner on the table. (Here's the third quality about risotto I love: you've got to open a bottle of wine to deglaze the pan, so you might as well enjoy a glass while the cooking is under way.)

RECIPES:

— TIME-SAVER RISOTTO   201

— TRIPLE-CARROT RISOTTO   202

— RISOTTO CARBONARA   205

— PAELLA RISOTTO   206

— FRENCH ONION ARANCINI   208

— "SHRIMP AND GRITS" RISOTTO   210

TIME-SAVER RISOTTO

NOTES / INGREDIENTS / METHOD:

You may have heard that the only way to make risotto is to devote yourself to standing and stirring in a little liquid at a time, but this method proves that wrong. By cooking the rice at a full boil, the bubbling and convection action of the cooking liquid stirs the rice and achieves the same result: creamy risotto, but with almost no standing at attention.

¼ cup extra-virgin olive oil
1 white onion, finely chopped
1 teaspoon salt
1 cup Arborio rice

1 cup white wine
4½ cups chicken stock
4 tablespoons (½ stick) butter
½ cup shavings of Parmesan cheese

ADD RICE TO THE ONION

Heat the oil in a large saucepan over medium-high heat and add the onion. Season with salt, and sweat the onion until it is translucent. Add the rice and stir for 2 minutes, until it begins to look translucent as well. Add the wine and stir, then allow it to reduce until it is almost gone.

Turn the heat up to high and add all of the stock. The liquid will come to a boil and "stir" the risotto for you, though you may want to stir occasionally. After boiling for 18 to 20 minutes, the rice should be almost done. Turn the heat down to a simmer and stir regularly for a few minutes to release the starch: this will make your risotto creamy. When the rice is tender but still has a little bite, turn off the heat and stir in the butter and Parmesan. Serve immediately, or spread out on a sheet pan to let cool and refrigerate to use later.

SIDE BY SIDE, COMPARED TO TRADITIONAL RISOTTO

OUR TIME-SAVER RISOTTO WAS CREAMY AND DELICIOUS

101

TRIPLE-CARROT RISOTTO

2 to 4

NOTES / INGREDIENTS / METHOD:

This vegetarian risotto is a two-pan pickup, keeping after-dinner cleanup to a minimum. We highlight carrots in three ways here: by folding carrot puree into the risotto, by topping it with browned-butter carrots, and by garnishing with carrot curls and tops. The puree turns the risotto a bright orange, and the cooked and raw carrots add great texture to the dish.

1 bunch carrots, with tops	1 recipe **Time-Saver Risotto** (page 201)
1 lemon	¼ cup freshly grated Parmesan cheese, or more to taste
Kosher salt	
2 tablespoons olive oil	¼ cup pomegranate seeds
3 tablespoons butter	Balsamic vinegar or pomegranate molasses
4 sage leaves	
½ cup walnuts	

CARROT PUREE TURNS IT VIBRANT ORANGE

Peel the carrots. Take the widest carrot from the bunch and cut it in half crosswise. Using the vegetable peeler, shave wide strips from the top half of the carrot. Add the carrot strips to ice water and place in the refrigerator; they will curl. Remove the top leaves from the carrot tops, add to cold water, and refrigerate as well.

Cut the remaining carrots into coins about ⅓ inch thick. Place in a large saucepan along with a ½-inch-wide strip of lemon peel and just enough water to cover. Add 1 teaspoon salt. Bring to a boil over high heat, turn down the heat, and simmer for about 10 minutes, or until the carrots are mostly tender but still a little al dente. Remove one third of the carrots from the liquid using a slotted spoon, and continue simmering the rest.

Add the olive oil and 2 tablespoons of the butter to a medium sauté pan and place over medium heat. When the butter foams, add the sage leaves and fry until crisp and the butter is a nutty brown, about 2 minutes. Transfer the leaves to a paper towel. Crumble the walnuts into the pan, and let them toast a bit. Add the reserved carrots to the pan, cut the lemon in half, and squeeze in the juice of one half. Take the pan off the heat.

Drain the carrots in the saucepan when they are fully tender, saving 1 cup of the cooking liquid. Put the carrots into a blender and puree, adding a splash of the cooking liquid if necessary to help achieve a smooth puree. Add the remaining 1 tablespoon butter and puree until smooth.

Pour the risotto into the saucepan you cooked the carrots in and warm it over medium-high heat. Add the carrot puree to the risotto, along with a splash of the carrot cooking liquid if needed to loosen it up. Stir in the Parmesan, season to taste with salt, and squeeze on the juice from the other lemon half.

Plate the risotto in a large serving dish. Top with the sautéed walnuts and carrots, and drizzle with some of the browned butter from the pan. Sprinkle the pomegranate seeds over the risotto, and add the carrot curls from the refrigerator, along with some of the carrot tops. Add the fried sage leaves. Sprinkle on more Parmesan as desired, and serve immediately.

GREAT FOR BOTH VEGETARIANS AND ~~MEAT~~ MEAT EATERS

RISOTTO CARBONARA

4

102

NOTES / INGREDIENTS / METHOD:

Our carbonara recipe (see page 134) uses super-soft scrambled eggs instead of the traditional raw egg that gets cooked by the hot pasta. We wanted to continue to riff on the idea of what carbonara could be— and why not use risotto as the vehicle instead? We popped this version under the broiling element for a minute to barely set the egg yolks, then finished the dish with a squeeze of lemon for a hit of acidity. This is pure comfort food.

8 ounces various fresh mushrooms (such as cremini, shiitake, trumpet)
8 ounces pancetta or bacon
Extra-virgin olive oil
2 thyme sprigs
Kosher salt
Freshly ground black pepper

Juice of 1 lemon
1 recipe Time-Saver Risotto (page 201)
Chicken broth or water, as needed
4 egg yolks
¼ cup chopped chives
Grated Parmesan cheese

Clean the mushrooms with a damp paper towel and slice in half. Cut the pancetta into small dice. Place the pancetta in a wide sauté pan set over medium heat, add a touch of olive oil, and render the pancetta until sizzling vigorously. Add the mushrooms to the pan, setting them in cut side down. Strip the thyme leaves from the stem, add them to the pan, and increase the heat to medium-high. Stir the mushrooms as they release their liquid and it evaporates; when the liquid cooks off and the pan is dry, the mushrooms will caramelize. Season them with salt and pepper, and finish with a bit more olive oil and half of the lemon juice. Keep warm.

Preheat the oven to broil.

Place the risotto in a large saucepan over medium-low heat and add a splash of broth or water; you don't need to cook the risotto, you are simply reheating it. The risotto should be loose and very hot; add more broth or water if necessary.

Transfer the hot risotto to an ovenproof serving dish. Gently top with the egg yolks. Scatter the mushrooms and bacon over the dish, leaving the yolks uncovered. Drizzle with a bit more olive oil. Broil the dish for a few seconds, to partially set the yolks. Sprinkle on the rest of the lemon juice, the chives, a dash of black pepper, and the Parmesan.

CARAMELIZE
THE MUSHROOMS

103   PAELLA RISOTTO   4

NOTES / INGREDIENTS / METHOD:

Our house is a great neighborhood gathering space, and each year we throw a big paella party; people come and go, grabbing a plate whenever it suits them. This paella risotto combines chicken, shrimp, clams, and sausage, all cooked in one pan, with our time-saving risotto standing in for the traditional rice preparation.

2 tablespoons extra-virgin olive oil

1 link **Spanish chorizo sausage**, sliced into ¼-inch coins

4 chicken thighs

Kosher salt

½ pound shell-on shrimp

1 red bell pepper

½ white onion

4 large garlic cloves

Generous pinch of saffron

4 fresh bay leaves

1 recipe **Time-Saver Risotto** (page 201)

Chicken stock or water, as needed

6 cherrystone clams

½ **Meyer lemon**, sliced into thin rings

3 whole calamari, cleaned and cut into rings

¼ cup parsley leaves

SEAR THE CHICKEN TO CRISP THE SKIN

Preheat the oven to 400°F. Heat the oil in a large ovenproof sauté pan that fits in the oven set over medium heat. Add the chorizo and sauté 5 minutes, until rendered and slightly browned. Remove with a slotted spoon and set aside. Pat the chicken dry with a paper towel and season with salt. Add to the pan, skin side down, and sear the chicken for 10 minutes, turn the pieces over, and cook for 8 more minutes. The chicken should be cooked through. Remove from the pan.

Insert a knife into the shrimp and split up the back toward the tail, stopping just before the tail. Remove the vein, if visible.

Place the bell pepper, onion, and garlic in a food processor and finely chop. Add the chopped vegetables to the sauté pan along with the saffron and bay leaves, and sweat the vegetables for 5 to 10 minutes, until soft and very aromatic.

Add the risotto to the vegetables in the pan. If the risotto is dry or tight, loosen it with a little chicken stock or water. Nestle the chicken into the risotto. Arrange the clams in the risotto around the edge. Season the shrimp with salt and add it to the pan, followed by the chorizo. Top the paella with the Meyer lemon rings. Bake for 15 minutes. Remove and add the calamari to the top of the paella, and place back in the oven for 2 minutes more, until the calamari is cooked, opaque but still tender. Top with the parsley leaves and serve.

I LOVE THAT THIS RECIPE HAPPENS IN ONE PAN

FRENCH ONION ARANCINI

4 to 6

FORM THE ARANCINI

NOTES / INGREDIENTS / METHOD:

Two things I love: French onion soup and arancini. Both have been perfected over the years, but one day in the Test Kitchen we had occasion to develop a new concept that uses the best of both. As we were looking at the spread of ingredients, trying to come up with something new, we thought: "Why not combine them?" We used the soup flavors—caramelized onion, wine, and molten Gruyère—as a stuffing for the arancini. These cheesy, oniony fried rice balls look great on a serving platter and are a lot of fun for a party.

1 tablespoon butter
1 tablespoon extra-virgin olive oil
1 white onion, finely chopped
4 thyme sprigs
1 cup red wine
¼ cup chicken stock
2 tablespoons balsamic vinegar
Kosher salt
Freshly ground black pepper

2 tablespoons finely chopped parsley
8 ounces Gruyère cheese
½ recipe Time-Saver Risotto, chilled (page 201)
2 cups panko breadcrumbs
Grapeseed or canola oil, for frying
Grated Parmesan cheese
5 fresh sage leaves
2 rosemary sprigs

Add the butter and olive oil to a medium saucepan over medium heat, then add the chopped onion and 1 thyme sprig. Cook, stirring, for 10 or more minutes, until the onion caramelizes to a deep, even brown. Add the wine, stock, and vinegar, and allow to reduce until it's syrupy. Season with salt, pepper, and the parsley. Remove the thyme sprig. Spread the onion on a plate to let it cool, and place in the refrigerator to chill.

Cut the Gruyère into ½-inch cubes. Place a golf-ball-size portion of risotto in the palm of your hand and flatten it. Add a dab (around ¼ teaspoon) of the onion in the center of the risotto, then top with a piece of the cheese. Form the risotto around the cheese and shape into a ball, ensuring that the cheese and onion are fully sealed.

FOLD THE RISOTTO AROUND THE CHEESE

In a food processor or blender, grind half of the breadcrumbs into a fine powder. Mix with the remaining breadcrumbs. Drop the rice balls into the breadcrumbs and toss until well coated.

Preheat the oven to 200°F.

Heat 3 inches of grapeseed oil in a pot, at least 5 inches deep, over medium-high heat to 375°F. Carefully add as many risotto balls as will fit comfortably into the oil and fry for about 4 minutes, or until golden brown. Remove to a paper towel–lined plate. Sprinkle some Parmesan and salt over the balls while they are hot. Transfer to the oven to keep them warm. Continue to fry the rest of the rice balls, putting them into the oven to stay warm. When the last balls are done, fry the sage leaves and rosemary sprigs for 3 to 4 minutes until crisp. Strip the leaves from the rosemary stems, then scatter both herbs over the balls as a garnish.

THE FLAVORS OF FRENCH ONION SOUP IN A BITE

105 "SHRIMP AND GRITS" RISOTTO

4

NOTES / INGREDIENTS / METHOD:

While trying out risotto recipes in the Test Kitchen, we asked ourselves, "What is rice?" After chatting for a few minutes, we landed on the idea that rice is really like any other grain. Though my love for grits runs deep (see pages 243–47), I wanted to play with a new version of shrimp and grits. We brought the same flavors as you find in this traditional Southern dish, but used risotto as the starch instead. You'll love the results.

OLD BAY
+
SEAFOOD
=
CLASSIC

8 ounces andouille sausage
½ white onion
2 garlic cloves
½ pound shell-on shrimp
3 cups chicken stock
2 thyme sprigs
Extra-virgin olive oil
1 teaspoon paprika
1 tablespoon Old Bay seasoning
1 fresh bay leaf

2 tablespoons all-purpose flour
Juice of ½ lemon
Kosher salt
1 recipe Time-Saver Risotto (page 201)
¼ cup parsley leaves
2 tablespoons finely minced chives
Freshly ground black pepper
Shavings of Parmesan cheese

Cut a slit down the side of the sausages and remove the meat from the casing. Cut the sausage meat into small dice. Finely chop the onion and garlic.

Shell and devein the shrimp, reserving the shells. Pour the stock into a large saucepan and add the shrimp shells and the thyme. Set over medium heat to simmer and form a shrimp-flavored stock.

Heat a medium saucepan with a drizzle of olive oil over medium heat. Add the sausage and sauté until browned on all sides. Add the onion and cook, stirring occasionally, until the mixture is a rich brown and very aromatic. Add the garlic, paprika, Old Bay seasoning, and bay leaf to the saucepan. Stir, sprinkling in the flour, and cook for 3 minutes.

RECIPE CONTINUES

A COMFORTING, ELEGANT DINNER

Strain the stock and discard the shrimp shells. Slowly add 1½ cups of the shrimp stock to the sausage mixture, whisking to avoid forming clumps. Bring the pan to a boil, then lower the heat and simmer until the sauce thickens. Add the shrimp to the sauce to gently cook it through, a few minutes, then add the lemon juice. Season to taste with salt, and turn off the heat.

Place the risotto into a saucepan and reheat over medium heat, adding a bit of the shrimp stock to loosen it. Stir; the risotto should be hot and smooth.

Plate the risotto on a serving dish. Top with the shrimp mixture from the pan. Garnish with the parsley and chives, and a drizzle of olive oil, a sprinkling of pepper, and Parmesan shavings. Serve immediately.

THE SAUCE IS DELICIOUS WITH THE RISOTTO TO SOAK IT UP

SIDES & VEGETABLES

When I moved to California a few years ago, I knew that things would be different from living in an apartment in New York City. We would be much closer to Tolan's family, in her hometown of Mill Valley, just outside San Francisco. I likely wouldn't have to trek through snow on a regular basis, and I would have more space to call my own. The outstanding produce was another blessing—some of the best food in the country.

The Central Valley of California has the ideal climate and soil for a wide variety of fruits and vegetables, and so we are spoiled in being able to enjoy so much of it. The salads and vegetables in this chapter celebrate the flavors and textures of great produce. Of course, we couldn't resist the Test Kitchen temptation to get a little creative here, too.

The Double-Creamed Spinach (page 232) completely changed how I make this dish—or any other creamy greens. The Fronion Rings (page 252)—onion rings coated with french fries—were a true Test Kitchen accomplishment: I almost want to have an artist draw one so we could hang a picture of it on the wall. It took a lot of science and testing to get it right, but it was worth every minute.

These salads and vegetable dishes pair well with a variety of recipes in this book, or you could make a few of them for a fresh meal on their own.

The dishes in this section mean a lot to me. Growing up in South Carolina, I ate a lot of my grandmother's cooking—she was known as Florence Mama. I have warm memories of watching her cook, and even more memories of eating her comforting, delicious food. She was an inspiration for a lot of what is in this section, even as we pushed the envelope and weren't afraid to question tradition while still respecting it. In short, it is important to honor the past but also look to the future. We added a California spin to make some of these recipes fresher and more enjoyable year-round.

While my grandmother would swear by one version of black-eyed peas, we made three, one of which is a vegan chili. She had some of the creamiest grits in town, but we came up with three versions, including one that uses popcorn. The Oysters Rockefeller (page 234) and the Extra-Light Cornbread (page 248) are two other classic recipes that we gave a bit of a twist, and we're sure you'll want to make them over and over again.

At the end of the day, these recipes are about respecting what we know and love but not being afraid to treat them a little differently. I hope you'll enjoy them.

RECIPES:

- SUMMER PANZANELLA 216
- ARTICHOKES WITH CURRY
  COURT-BOUILLON AIOLI 218
- SALAD NIÇOISE CARPACCIO 220
- TUNA CONFIT DRESSING 222
- CAESAR SALAD WITH ANCHOVY-PARMESAN
  POTATO CROUTONS 223
- CAESAR DRESSING 225
- LOADED ICEBERG WEDGE SALAD 226
- CARMELIZED BRUSSELS SPROUTS
  WITH PANCETTA 228
- HERB-ROASTED WILD MUSHROOMS
  WITH RED WINE AND CREAM 230
- DOUBLE-CREAMED SPINACH WITH
  FRIED ONIONS 232
- OYSTERS ROCKEFELLER WITH
  DOUBLE-CREAMED SPINACH 234

RECIPES:

- CLASSIC BLACK-EYED PEAS WITH
    HAM HOCK 236
- BLACK-EYED PEA AND CHARRED
    VEGETABLE CHILI 238
- CHILE POWDER 241
- FRIED BLACK-EYED PEAS 241
- TOMATO AND BLACK-EYED PEA SALAD 242
- CREAMY CAROLINA GRITS 243
- POPCORN GRITS WITH
    CARAMELIZED MUSHROOMS 244
- FRESH CORN POBLANO "GRITS" 246
- EXTRA-LIGHT CORNBREAD 248
- FRONION RINGS 252

SUMMER PANZANELLA

4 to 6

THE TOMATO
VINAIGRETTE
SHOULD BE SMOOTH

I LOVE THE RUSTIC
LOOK OF TORN
BREAD

NOTES / INGREDIENTS / METHOD:

Panzanella is essentially a bread salad with a lot of fresh produce, so it's the perfect summer dish. Let the farmers' market dictate what you include, depending on what looks delicious at the time. In this case, we added peaches and corn for their pops of sweetness. Also, you roast two of the beets here and shave one to serve it raw. As long as you use produce that's great, this will be a refreshing side for summer nights at the grill.

3 red beets	**1 peach**
¼ cup extra-virgin olive oil, plus more as needed	**1 ear of corn, husked and silks removed**
2 ripe red heirloom tomatoes	**¼ red onion**
Kosher salt	**Freshly ground black pepper**
2 tablespoons red wine vinegar	**Niçoise olives**
½ loaf sourdough bread (great way to use day-old)	**Fresh herbs, such as marjoram, basil, Thai basil, mint**
5 ripe tomatoes of various colors and sizes	**⅓ cup Homemade Fresh Ricotta (page 57)**
1 cucumber	**A few chive stems, cut in half, for garnish**

Preheat the oven to 350°F. Lightly coat 2 beets in a little olive oil and set on a sheet of foil. Wrap them loosely, but fold all the edges shut so they're encased. Roast for 35 minutes, or until you can insert a knife easily into them. Once cool enough to handle, pinch and rub the skins off the beets: they should slide off easily. Shave the third beet using a mandoline.

Cut the red heirloom tomatoes in half and sprinkle generously with salt. Let them sit for a few minutes, then place in a blender. Add the vinegar and ¼ cup olive oil, and blend until smooth. Refrigerate the dressing until ready to use.

Tear the bread into bite-size pieces. You want to have a rustic look, so don't use a knife. Heat a large sauté pan over medium heat and coat with a little olive oil. Add the bread pieces and toast in one layer, tossing until they are crisp on the outside, but still have some chew. Do this in batches, if necessary.

Cut the tomatoes into both wedges and slices for a variety of shapes, and place in a large mixing bowl. Slice the cucumber in half lengthwise, then diagonally into thick slices. Cut the roasted beets and the peach into wedges. Slice the kernels from the corn. Cut the red onion into thin slices, then break into smaller pieces.

Add the dressing to the vegetables and toss. Add the toasted bread, and toss again. Season with salt, pepper, and a little additional olive oil. Arrange the vegetables on a serving platter, and top with the shaved raw beet, olives, and herbs. Add dollops of ricotta on top and lay on a few chive stems. Sprinkle on a little more salt, pepper, and olive oil, if desired.

ARTICHOKES WITH CURRY COURT-BOUILLON AIOLI

NOTES / INGREDIENTS / METHOD:

We spend a lot of time thinking about where flavor goes when foods are cooked, and how to avoid pouring that flavor down the drain. Poaching artichokes in a vegetable-packed liquid instead of water, for example, creates a savory court bouillon that can be repurposed as a dipping sauce for the artichokes. And there is no need to waste the poaching vegetables once the artichokes are cooked; turn them into an aioli for dipping. This is an easy technique that can be used in countless other applications.

ARTICHOKES AND COURT BOUILLON
2 leeks
2 carrots
3 lemons
1 head of garlic
5 bay leaves
5 thyme sprigs
1 tablespoon whole peppercorns
1 cup dry white wine
4 globe artichokes

Kosher salt
Flaky sea salt
Extra-virgin olive oil

AIOLI
3 eggs
1 cup grapeseed or vegetable oil
1 teaspoon kosher salt
Juice of ½ lemon
3 teaspoons curry powder

Prepare the artichokes Slice the leeks into rings up to the dark green leaves and rinse them in a bowl of cold water to remove the sand. Cut the carrots into 1-inch-thick pieces, and slice the lemons into thin rounds. Lightly crush the garlic. Place the vegetables in a large pot along with the bay leaves, thyme, and peppercorns. Fill with room-temperature water and add half of the wine. Put the artichokes in the pot to make sure they fit and are covered by the liquid, then remove them. Place the pot on medium heat and bring the liquid to a boil, then reduce to a simmer.

Add the rest of the wine and season the liquid with salt until it tastes pleasantly like seawater. Add the artichokes, and place a large plate on top of them to keep them submerged. Simmer gently for about 45 minutes, until a paring knife can be inserted into the bottom of the artichokes with just a bit of resistance. Turn the heat off and allow the artichokes to cool down in the court bouillon; they will continue to absorb flavor as they cool.

FLAVOR THE
LIQUID WITH
VEGETABLES,
GARLIC, AND
HERBS

Prepare the aioli Remove about half of the poaching vegetables from the court bouillon and place in a blender. Puree to a smooth applesauce consistency; if necessary, add some of the cooking liquid to loosen the mixture. While you let the mixture cool down a bit, separate the eggs. When the mixture is warm but no longer hot, add 1 whole egg plus 2 yolks, then blend to incorporate. (Use the 2 egg whites for another recipe.) Slowly drizzle in the grapeseed oil with the blender running to emulsify the mixture. Season with salt, lemon juice, and curry powder.

Once the artichokes have cooled, remove them from the poaching liquid. Trim off the stems. Place the artichokes in a serving dish, and garnish with any extra vegetables from the court boulllon. Sprinkle with flaky sea salt and drizzle with a little olive oil. Serve with the aioli.

DRIZZLE OIL INTO THE BLENDER

SALAD NIÇOISE CARPACCIO

4 to 6

NOTES / INGREDIENTS / METHOD:

Instead of the usual seared tuna, we prepare it in two ways here: as a dressing made from a confit of tuna, and as a tuna carpaccio that is the focus of the salad. The raw tuna provides the base and the dollops of tuna confit dressing contribute creaminess. We also use both roasted tomatoes and fresh cherry tomatoes, bringing two different textures and versions of the same ingredient. By deliberately building the layers of this composed salad on a serving platter, you create a truly artistic presentation to impress your guests.

2 Roma (plum) tomatoes
5 fingerling potatoes
Extra-virgin olive oil
Kosher salt
4 ounces green beans
6 ounces sushi-grade tuna
Tuna Confit Dressing (recipe follows)
2 soft-boiled eggs, cut in half
¼ cup cherry tomatoes
¼ fennel bulb, thinly sliced

6 mixed olives (green, black, Niçoise)
5 Sicilian caperberries (optional)
1 radish, thinly shaved (optional)
2 teaspoons chopped fennel fronds (optional)
3 anchovy fillets (optional)
1 cup mixed small greens (microgreens, tarragon leaves, basil buds, pansies, fennel fronds)
Freshly ground black pepper

POUND THE TUNA SO IT'S ALMOST TRANSPARENT

Preheat the oven to 400°F. Cut the tomatoes and potatoes in half lengthwise, place on a sheet pan, and drizzle with a little olive oil and salt. Roast in the oven for about 25 minutes. Meanwhile, blanch the green beans in salted boiling water for 2 minutes, then drain and plunge into an ice bath to stop the cooking.

Cut the sushi-grade tuna into two pieces. Cut a large sheet of plastic wrap and lay on a work surface. Drizzle with a little olive oil and set the tuna on top. Drizzle the tuna with a little more olive oil and cover with another large sheet of plastic. Using a heavy pan, gently pound the tuna to make it into a thin sheet; you want it to be so thin that it's almost transparent. Repeat with the other piece of tuna, then gently tear the pounded tuna into a few 2-inch pieces.

Lay pieces of the tuna carpaccio on a large serving platter, and arrange dollops of the tuna confit dressing around the edge. Scatter the roasted tomatoes and potatoes atop the carpaccio, add the halved eggs, then the green beans, cherry tomatoes, and fennel slices. Add the mixed olives, caperberries, radish, fennel fronds, and anchovies, if using, then arrange the small greens on the salad as well. Finish with a drizzle of olive oil, and salt and pepper to taste.

TUNA CONFIT DRESSING

1 (6-ounce) piece yellowfin tuna
1 head of garlic
1 rosemary sprig
1 teaspoon whole peppercorns
¾ fennel bulb, quartered
2 dried chiles de árbol
Grapeseed or canola oil
¼ cup sour cream

¼ cup mayonnaise
2 tablespoons Dijon mustard
1 small dill pickle, chopped
¼ cup parsley leaves, chopped
1 tablespoon drained capers
Zest from 1 lemon
Kosher salt
Freshly ground black pepper

POACH THE TUNA IN FLAVORED OIL

Place the tuna in a medium saucepan. Slice the top off of the head of garlic, exposing the cloves, and add to the saucepan along with the rosemary sprig, peppercorns, fennel chunks, and chiles. Cover with the grapeseed oil, and turn the heat to medium-low. Using a thermometer, bring the temperature of the oil up to 150°F and maintain it there for 10 minutes, poaching the tuna. Lift out the tuna, letting the oil drain off, and set in a bowl to cool. Discard the garlic and seasonings.

Combine the sour cream, mayonnaise, and mustard in a bowl. Mix in the chopped pickle and parsley along with the capers and lemon zest. Break up the cooled confit tuna and add that as well. Mix well and season with salt and pepper.

CAESAR SALAD WITH ANCHOVY-PARMESAN POTATO CROUTONS

NOTES / INGREDIENTS / METHOD:

What makes a Caesar salad special? To me, it's about striking the perfect balance between fresh romaine and flavorful dressing, with croutons for crunch. We substituted crispy potatoes for the croutons—and while we were at it, we flavored them with two of the best parts of a Caesar, the Parmesan and anchovy. The potatoes absorb the dressing terrifically and bring a welcome change to this classic salad. The dressing is presented here separately, as we use it in a few other recipes in this book; after all, you just can't go wrong with anchovies and garlic.

8 ounces new potatoes (approximately 8 to 10 golf-ball-size potatoes)

½ cup plus 1 tablespoon extra-virgin olive oil

1 teaspoon sea salt, plus more to taste

4 bay leaves

2 anchovy fillets, drained, patted dry, and oil reserved

1 garlic clove

6 tablespoons freshly grated Parmesan cheese, plus more for garnish

Freshly ground black pepper

1 pound mixed lettuces (romaine, gem, and butter)

Caesar Dressing (recipe follows), as desired

Shavings of Parmesan cheese

Preheat the oven to 425°F.

Rinse the potatoes and slice in half. Place on a sheet pan and toss with ¼ cup of the oil, 1 teaspoon sea salt, and the bay leaves. Make sure the potatoes are skin side down on the pan. Roast for 25 minutes, until nice and crisp. Discard the bay leaves.

Finely chop together the anchovies, garlic, and a pinch of sea salt, then mash with the side of your knife until it's a paste. Transfer to a large bowl and add ¼ cup oil, 4 tablespoons of the Parmesan, and a drop of the reserved anchovy oil. Whisk together, and season with pepper.

RECIPE CONTINUES

CRISPY POTATOES ACT AS CROUTONS

Fill a large bowl with cold water, and place the lettuces in the water. Gently agitate the leaves to loosen any dirt, which will sink to the bottom while the leaves float on top. Transfer the leaves to towels and gently pat dry. (Salad spinners tend to bruise lettuce.) Keep small leaves whole, and tear large leaves into generous-size pieces.

Toss the potatoes in the anchovy-cheese paste, then put them back in the oven for another 5 to 7 minutes, until the cheese melts. Toss with the remaining 2 tablespoons Parmesan.

Smear a generous layer of dressing on the inside of a large mixing bowl—this helps to incorporate the dressing evenly. Add the lettuce leaves to the bowl, and toss to coat the leaves with dressing. Toss in more dressing, if desired. Add a few shavings of Parmesan cheese, a sprinkling of black pepper, and the remaining 1 tablespoon oil. Place the dressed leaves on a platter, and top with the potato croutons and a final shower of grated Parmesan. Serve immediately.

CAESAR DRESSING

Makes about 2 cups

6 anchovy fillets	1 cup grapeseed or canola oil
5 garlic cloves	1 tablespoon extra-virgin olive oil
1 whole egg plus 2 yolks	¼ cup grated Parmesan cheese
Juice of 1 lemon	Sea or kosher salt
1 tablespoon Dijon mustard	Freshly ground black pepper

Place the anchovies, garlic cloves, the egg and yolks, lemon juice, mustard, and a splash of water in a blender and mix. With the blender running, slowly pour in the grapeseed oil to make a thick dressing. Add the olive oil, Parmesan cheese, and salt and pepper to taste, and blend. Refrigerate the dressing if you will not be using it right away.

USE LEFTOVER DRESSING
IN THE CAESAR SALAD
"DEVILED EGGS" (page 104)

112 LOADED ICEBERG WEDGE SALAD

ADD WHATEVER
EXTRAS
YOU'D LIKE

NOTES / INGREDIENTS / METHOD:

There are no limits on what to add to a wedge salad—in fact, we ended up adding watermelon cubes as a refreshing balance to the tangy dressing. But do take the time to deliberately place the ingredients in the salad. Having a well-composed dish adds only an extra minute or two and satisfies the eat-with-your-eyes-first inclination.

4 strips of bacon	Kosher salt
3 bay leaves	Freshly ground black pepper
3 rosemary sprigs	3 heads of baby iceberg lettuce
½ cup mayonnaise	2 ripe tomatoes
½ cup sour cream	Extra-virgin olive oil
¼ cup buttermilk	
½ teaspoon onion powder	POSSIBLE EXTRAS
½ teaspoon garlic powder	Shaved radishes
Juice of 1 lemon	Watercress
1 bunch of chives	Cherry tomatoes
½ cup Maytag blue cheese	Watermelon cubes

Cut the bacon into ½-inch strips. Fry in a medium sauté pan over medium heat along with the bay leaves and rosemary sprigs. When the bacon is crisp, drain it on a paper towel–lined plate.

In a mixing bowl, combine the mayonnaise and sour cream, then mix in the buttermilk. Add the onion powder, garlic powder, and lemon juice. Finely chop the chives from the base up, stopping about 2 inches from the top; save these chive *batons* to garnish the salad. Crumble most of the blue cheese into the dressing, reserving some for a garnish. Mix the dressing and add salt and freshly ground black pepper to taste.

Cut each iceberg head into 4 wedges. Cut the tomatoes into large wedges. Smear some dressing on the bottom of a large serving dish. Arrange the iceberg and tomato wedges on top of the dressing. Crumble the bacon on top, add any desired extras, then finish with a bit more of the dressing, a drizzle of olive oil, and a sprinkle of salt and freshly ground black pepper. Garnish with the chive *batons* and remaining blue cheese. Serve immediately.

113

CARAMELIZED BRUSSELS SPROUTS WITH PANCETTA

4 to 6

NOTES / INGREDIENTS / METHOD:

Pancetta is pork belly cured in sugar, salt, and spices and then air-dried, whereas bacon is cured and then smoked. We wanted to let the Brussels sprouts shine, so we chose pancetta over bacon to avoid a too-smoky taste. Some people have strong feelings about Brussels sprouts; they always used to be overcooked and mushy, but ours stay crunchy when roasted and have a great caramelized flavor. Serve this at your next holiday dinner.

PANCETTA ADDS FLAVOR WITHOUT SMOKE

2 pounds Brussels sprouts
Extra-virgin olive oil
4 (¼-inch-thick) slices pancetta
3 shallots
2 garlic cloves
Kosher salt
Freshly ground black pepper
6 thyme sprigs

4 slices good sourdough bread
8 fresh sage leaves
1 rosemary sprig, cut into 1-inch
**   pieces**
½ cup balsamic vinegar
½ cup chicken stock
2 tablespoons butter
Grated Parmesan cheese

Preheat the oven to 400°F. Cut the Brussels sprouts in half, put them on a sheet pan in a single layer, and coat them with a little olive oil. Roughly chop the pancetta and add to the sprouts. Peel the shallots, cut them in half, and add to the sprouts. Cut the garlic cloves in half and add to the pan along with a generous sprinkling of salt, pepper, and 3 of the thyme sprigs. Roast until the sprouts are caramelized, about 25 minutes, stirring midway.

Cut the bread into ¼-inch dice. Coat a large sauté pan with some olive oil and place over medium heat. Add the bread to the pan along with the sage, rosemary, and remaining 3 thyme sprigs. Cook, stirring, until the bread is toasted well.

Simmer the balsamic vinegar, chicken stock, 2 tablespoons olive oil, the butter, and a pinch of salt in a small saucepan over medium heat until it reaches a syrupy consistency. Set aside.

While the sprouts are still hot, use a spoon to break apart the shallots a bit, then transfer all the vegetables to a large mixing bowl. Season to taste with salt. Pour the balsamic glaze over the sprouts and toss. Sprinkle a little Parmesan over the sprouts, then transfer them to a serving dish. Top with the diced bread and more grated Parmesan, and serve immediately.

TOAST THE BREAD IN A SAUTÉ PAN

I LOVE THE CRISPY LEAVES

114

HERB-ROASTED WILD MUSHROOMS WITH RED WINE AND CREAM

4 to 6

NOTES / INGREDIENTS / METHOD:

We're lucky to have great wild mushrooms in northern California in the fall. Roasting the mushrooms caramelizes their edges, creating nice textures and deep flavors, while the wine and cream sauce brings both acidity and richness. You can serve this side dish with everything from Super-Crisp Roast Chicken (page 69) to Seared Brined Pork Chops (page 151) and salmon.

2 pounds assorted mushrooms (such as cremini, oyster, shiitake, chanterelle, black trumpet)
Extra-virgin olive oil
6 bay leaves
4 thyme sprigs
2 rosemary sprigs, cut into 1-inch pieces
3 shallots, 2 cut in half
Kosher salt
Freshly ground black pepper
1 tablespoon unsalted butter
1 teaspoon whole peppercorns
2 cups good red wine
¼ cup heavy cream
¼ cup arugula leaves

Preheat the oven to 450°F. Brush the mushrooms clean of any dirt and trim off any deep blemishes. Slice about ¼ inch thick. Put the mushrooms in one layer on one or more sheet pans (as necessary), and drizzle with a little olive oil. Add 4 bay leaves, the thyme and rosemary sprigs, and the 2 halved shallots. Season generously with salt and pepper. Roast about 15 minutes, until the mushrooms caramelize and are golden brown.

Slice the remaining shallot into rings and break the rings apart with your hands. Heat a small saucepan with the butter over medium heat. Add the shallot, 2 remaining bay leaves, the peppercorns, and 1 tablespoon olive oil. Cook the shallot, stirring, until a deep caramel brown. Add the wine and let the mixture reduce until it coats the back of a spoon, about 10 minutes. Add the cream and cook until it thickens again, about 2 minutes more. Season with salt to taste.

Transfer the roasted mushrooms to a serving dish, removing the bay leaves and herb stems, and drizzle with the sauce. Garnish with the arugula.

ROAST THE MUSHROOMS WITH HERBS

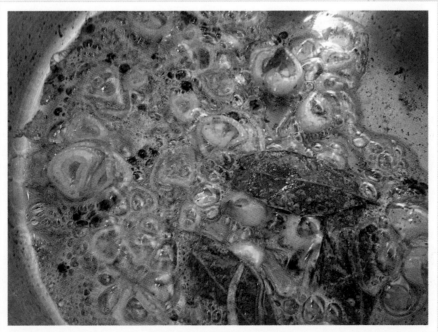

CARAMELIZE THE SHALLOTS

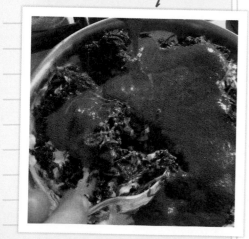

DOUBLE-CREAMED SPINACH WITH FRIED ONIONS

NOTE: HERBSAINT IS A LIQUEUR MADE IN NEW ORLEANS. THINK OF IT AS THE AMERICAN VERSION OF PERNOD. IT HAS A MINTY-ANISE FLAVOR.

THE NEON GREEN COLOR AMAZES ME EVERY TIME

NOTES / INGREDIENTS / METHOD:

With most creamed spinach, all you taste is the super-rich cream rather than the spinach itself. Instead of masking it, we wanted the spinach to shine. So, we used a béchamel base instead of cream, and pureed some of the spinach into the sauce (hence "double-creamed spinach"). We ended up with a creamed spinach that was not only packed with spinach flavor but also had the most amazing neon-green color. And this method of pureeing the vegetable to dress itself works just as well with kale–find it in our recipe for Pork Chops with Creamed Kale (page 155). See the recipe for Oysters Rockefeller (page 234), if you manage to have any creamed spinach left over.

1½ pounds fresh spinach, cleaned
2 large onions
5 tablespoons all-purpose flour
Kosher salt
Freshly ground pepper
Grapeseed or vegetable oil
1 fennel bulb

½ tablespoon extra-virgin olive oil
2 garlic cloves
¼ cup Herbsaint (see Note) *
1 cup whole milk
2 tablespoons butter
½ teaspoon grated nutmeg
⅓ cup freshly grated Parmesan cheese

Bring a large pot of generously salted water to a boil. Add the spinach, and as soon as it's wilted and tender, drain and run under cold water. When the spinach is cool enough to handle, squeeze out any excess water. If you have used whole spinach with long stems, roughly chop it. You should have 3 cups of chopped spinach.

Thinly slice 1 onion into thin disks, and break the disks into rings with your hands. Mix 2 tablespoons of the flour with a bit of salt and pepper, and toss the onion rings in the flour. Heat 1 inch of grapeseed oil to 350°F in a large, deep sauté pan or Dutch oven. Add a handful of onion rings to the oil, making sure they have room to move. Fry in the oil for 3 to 4 minutes, until golden brown. Transfer to a paper towel–lined plate. If desired, keep them warm in a 200°F oven.

Finely mince the fennel bulb and the remaining onion. Heat a large sauté pan over medium heat and glaze with the olive oil, then add the fennel, onion, garlic, and a few pinches of salt. Cook until the onion is translucent; you don't want it to brown. Add the remaining

3 tablespoons of flour and stir. When the flour has gathered up all the onion mixture, add the Herbsaint and bring to a boil. Let it reduce by half, then stir in the milk to make a béchamel. Season to taste with salt and pepper. Cook at a low simmer until the sauce thickens to the point where it coats the back of a spoon and drawing your finger down the spoon leaves a clear line.

Pour half of the béchamel into a blender with 1 cup of the spinach. Blend until completely smooth. Add the remaining 2 cups spinach to the pan containing the remaining béchamel, then pour in the spinach puree. Heat, stirring, and season with salt and pepper. Finish by stirring in the butter, nutmeg, and Parmesan. Transfer the creamed spinach to a serving dish, and top with the fried onion.

MY SON HAYDEN OFFERED A HELPING HAND

116 OYSTERS ROCKEFELLER WITH DOUBLE-CREAMED SPINACH

MAKES 24 PIECES

NOTES / INGREDIENTS / METHOD:

This recipe uses one of our favorites in this book, the Double-Creamed Spinach on page 232. I'll be impressed if you manage to have any leftover creamed spinach, but if you do, this New Orleans classic is a great use for it. We add bacon to our version to bring some smoke to the dish. You could leave it out, or use smoked olive oil to finish instead.

I LOVE THIS OLD-SCHOOL SERVING DISH

½ cup panko breadcrumbs

Extra-virgin olive oil

24 medium, sweet and briny oysters

½ cup **Double-Creamed Spinach** (page 232)

6 slices of bacon, cut into 1½-inch pieces

Coarse salt, for baking

Fennel pollen

Grated fresh horseradish (optional)

Smoked olive oil (optional)

3 lemons, cut into wedges

Preheat the oven to 500°F. Moisten the breadcrumbs with a little bit of olive oil.

Shuck the oysters. There is a top flat "lid" and a bottom cupped shell for each oyster. Insert the tip of an oyster knife into the hinge where the two shells come together in a point. Twist until the lid pops open. Pull the knife out and wipe the knife clean so you don't get mud in the oyster. Insert the knife back into the oyster from the opposite side of the hinge, lightly scraping against the top shell to disconnect the muscle. Then go under the oyster to cut the muscle on the bottom, and flip the oyster over onto the prettier side.

Top each oyster with a teaspoon of creamed spinach, a piece of bacon, and a bit of the breadcrumbs. Create a small mound of coarse salt on a baking sheet for each oyster to prevent them from tipping over. Nestle the oysters in the salt mounds, and bake until the bacon is cooked and the breadcrumbs brown.

Transfer the baked oysters to a serving platter and garnish with a sprinkle of fennel pollen. If desired, garnish with grated horseradish and a drizzle of smoked olive oil. Serve with lemon wedges.

TOP THE OYSTERS WITH DOUBLE-CREAMED SPINACH

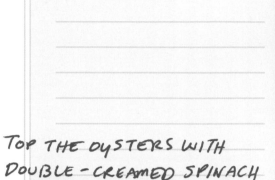

BREADCRUMBS MAKE THESE CRUNCHY

117 CLASSIC BLACK-EYED PEAS WITH HAM HOCK

6

CELERY
+
BELL
PEPPER
+
ONION
=
THE
HOLY
TRINITY

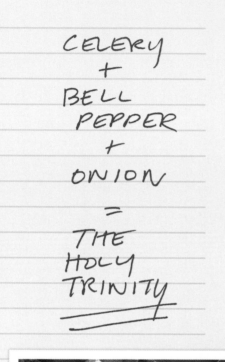

NOTES / INGREDIENTS / METHOD:

Black-eyed peas are a delicious, common side dish in the South, with origins in Africa. Tradition says that eating black-eyed peas on New Year's Day offers prosperity in the year to come, so you'll find this on a lot of tables on January 1. Take the time to soak the beans overnight in salted water. If you skip this step, they won't get creamy. To avoid throwing bean flavor down the drain, use just enough liquid for the beans to absorb and swell up. If you have any leftovers, see the Tomato and Black-Eyed Pea Salad (page 242).

2 cups dried black-eyed peas
Kosher salt
1 green bell pepper
1 white onion
3 long celery ribs
1½ tablespoons red chile flakes
2 tablespoons gumbo filé (ground sassafras; optional, but desirable)

2 fresh bay leaves
3 garlic cloves
Extra-virgin olive oil
1 ham hock, cut in half
Freshly ground black pepper
Juice of ½ lemon
½ cup chopped parsley

Four hours or more before cooking, soak the black-eyed peas in 6 cups of water with 3 teaspoons of salt. Store in the refrigerator if soaking overnight. Drain when ready to cook.

Roughly chop the bell pepper, half of the onion, and the celery, then add them to a food processor and process until well chopped. Add the chile flakes, gumbo filé, bay leaves, and garlic, and process until almost pureed but still a little chunky.

Heat 4 tablespoons of olive oil in a large pot over medium-high heat, then add the chopped vegetables. Cook, stirring, until they have shrunk almost in half, losing their moisture and concentrating their flavor. Add the ham hock. Continue to cook until the vegetables become very soft and brown, then add the black-eyed peas. Cover with 1½ quarts of water, bring to a boil, then reduce to a slow simmer. The beans will take about 1 hour to cook.

Season the beans with salt, pepper, and lemon juice. Stir in most of the parsley. Place the beans in a serving dish, and nestle the ham hock on top. Slice the remaining onion half into thin rings, and use to garnish the beans along with a sprinkling of the remaining parsley.

I COULD EAT THESE RIGHT OUT OF
THE POT — THEY BRING ME
BACK TO GROWING UP

118–120 BLACK-EYED PEA AND CHARRED VEGETABLE CHILI

6

NOTES / INGREDIENTS / METHOD:

This vegan chili was a fun dish to create. We used the same base as for the Classic Black-Eyed Peas (page 236), but instead of using a smoky ham hock, we relied on charred vegetables to build the layers of the chili. And since we had a vegan chili as our canvas, we came up with a vegan "sour cream," inspired by the Mexican rice-based drink *horchata*. Frying the black-eyed peas adds worthwhile crunch to the dish, as well. This chili would be fantastic on a cold day, and it easily serves a crowd, pleasing vegans and nonvegans alike.

CHILI

½ cup dried hominy
¾ cup black-eyed peas
½ cup yellow-eyed peas
Kosher salt
1 green bell pepper
1½ onions
3 celery ribs
1½ tablespoons red chile flakes
2 tablespoons gumbo filé (ground
  sassafras)
2 fresh bay leaves
3 garlic cloves
Olive oil
2 tablespoons Chile Powder
  (recipe follows)
¼ cup masa harina (cornmeal
  used for tortillas)
2 large tomatoes
2 poblano peppers
2 Jimmy Nardello peppers
  or red bell peppers
1 tablespoon cumin seeds
2 to 3 limes

TOFU-HORCHATA "SOUR CREAM"

3 limes
1 cup uncooked white rice
3 cinnamon sticks
⅓ cup almonds
½ block medium-firm tofu

CHILI GARNISHES

3 radishes, shaved
Cilantro sprigs
Sliced serrano chile
Chive blossoms
Fried Black-Eyed Peas (page 241)

SOAK THE RICE, LIME, CINNAMON, AND ALMONDS OVERNIGHT

The night before For the chili, place the hominy, black-eyed peas, and yellow-eyed peas in a bowl with 2 quarts of water and 4 teaspoons of salt; place in the refrigerator to double in size overnight. For the "sour cream," slice 1 of the limes and combine with the rice, cinnamon sticks, and almonds in a bowl. Pour in 2 cups of water and soak overnight in the refrigerator.

Make the chili Preheat the oven to broil. Roughly chop the bell pepper, the onion half, and the celery, then pulse in a food processor until finely chopped. Add the red chile flakes, gumbo filé, bay leaves, and garlic, and process until almost pureed. Coat the bottom of a large pot with some olive oil and set over medium heat. When the oil shimmers, add the chopped vegetables, and cook, stirring occasionally, to extract the moisture. Add the chile powder and stir in the masa harina.

Cut the tomatoes into large pieces. Also cut the remaining onion, the poblano peppers, and the Jimmy Nardello peppers into large pieces. Combine in a bowl and coat with olive oil and the cumin seeds. Put the vegetables on a sheet pan and broil for 15 minutes or until charred.

RECIPE CONTINUES

Peel off some of the charred skins from the broiled vegetables. Add them to a food processor and puree. Add the pureed vegetables to the pot along with a drizzle of olive oil.

Drain the soaked hominy, black-eyed peas, and yellow-eyed peas, and add to the pot. (If making the fried black-eyed peas garnish, set aside ¼ cup of soaked beans for that purpose.) Stir to combine. Cover the ingredients with water, bring to a boil, turn down to a simmer, and cook 45 minutes to 1 hour, until the beans are tender but still whole. Taste and season the chili with salt, lime juice, and more chile powder, as desired.

Make the tofu-horchata "sour cream" Remove the lime slices and cinnamon stick from the overnight-soaked mixture. Transfer the rice and almonds to a blender along with ½ cup of the soaking liquid. Process until smooth, then add the tofu and lime juice. Blend, taste, and adjust seasonings with additional salt and lime juice as desired.

To serve, top the bowls of the chili with the "sour cream," shaved radishes, cilantro sprigs, thin slices of serrano chile, chive blossoms, and fried black-eyed peas.

MAKE YOUR OWN
CHILE POWDER
AND USE THE
EXTRA IN OTHER
RECIPES

CHILE POWDER

Makes about ¼ cup

4 dried New Mexico chiles
2 teaspoons cumin seeds
2 teaspoons coriander seeds
2 teaspoons black peppercorns

2 teaspoons mustard seeds
2 teaspoons sumac
2 tablespoons paprika
1 cinnamon stick

Combine the New Mexico chiles, cumin and coriander seeds, peppercorns, mustard seeds, sumac, paprika, and cinnamon stick in a spice grinder. Process until fine.

FRIED BLACK-EYED PEAS

¼ cup overnight-soaked black-
    eyed peas
Grapeseed or canola oil, for frying

Masa harina, for dusting
Kosher salt
Chile Powder (recipe above)

Boil the soaked black-eyed peas in water for 10 to 15 minutes, until tender. Drain and dry them by rolling them in a bowl lined with paper towels. Heat 2 inches of oil in a saucepan with a few inches of clearance over medium-high heat. When the oil is 360°F, dust the peas with some masa harina, and fry until crisp and golden, 3 to 4 minutes. Drain on a paper towel–lined plate and season with salt and chile powder.

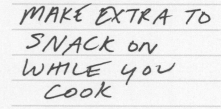

MAKE EXTRA TO SNACK ON WHILE YOU COOK

TOMATO AND BLACK-EYED PEA SALAD

4 to 6

BLEND
BLACK-EYED
PEAS WITH
MAYO FOR
THE DRESSING

NOTES / INGREDIENTS / METHOD:

If you manage to have leftover Classic Black-Eyed Peas (page 236), this salad is a refreshing way to use them up the next day. The peas are used in both the dressing and the salad.

2 cups Classic Black-Eyed Peas with Ham Hock (page 236)
½ cup mayonnaise
Kosher salt
Juice of 1 lemon

4 heirloom tomatoes
Flaky sea salt
Fresh basil leaves
Chive blossoms
Whole parsley leaves

In a blender, combine ½ cup peas with the mayonnaise and blend until smooth to make the dressing. Season to taste with kosher salt and lemon juice.

Slice the tomatoes, place the slices on a serving dish, and sprinkle with flaky sea salt. Top with the remaining peas, and drizzle the dressing over the plate. Garnish with basil leaves, chive blossoms, and parsley.

CREAMY CAROLINA GRITS

NOTES / INGREDIENTS / METHOD:

I'm from South Carolina, where grits are a staple item on the dinner table. In the 1990s, grits became a comfort food on menus around the country, even if you didn't call them that: whether you refer to them as grits or polenta really depends on where your family came from. Polenta is typically made with a finer grind of cornmeal than grits and ends up smoother, whereas grits tend to have a more toothsome texture, but both are really just cornmeal mush. This peasant dish goes to new heights if you use quality ground corn, so take the time to seek it out. Grits are a great complement to the Super-Crisp Roast Chicken (page 69).

2½ cups heavy cream
2½ cups whole milk
2 garlic cloves, smashed
4 thyme sprigs
4 fresh bay leaves

1 cup yellow cornmeal or polenta (not instant grits)
1½ tablespoons unsalted butter
¼ cup freshly grated Parmesan cheese
Kosher salt
Freshly ground black pepper

BUTTER AND PARMESAN FLAVOR THE GRITS

Add the cream, milk, garlic, thyme, and bay leaves to a large saucepan. Bring to a simmer over medium-low heat, and let simmer for 10 minutes to allow the flavors to infuse the liquid. Remove the herbs and garlic from the milk, turn the heat up to medium, and bring the liquid to a boil. Gradually rain in the cornmeal while whisking. With a wooden spoon or heatproof rubber spatula, continuously stir the grits, as the natural starch from the corn creates a film on the bottom of the pan that can burn.

Cook the grits for about 15 minutes, until thick and smooth with just a little bit of rough texture. The longer you cook them, the smoother they will be, but add a little milk or water to thin them if they get too thick for your taste. (Cornmeal also absorbs liquid differently depending on where it is from and how old it is.) Finish by stirring in the butter, Parmesan, and salt and pepper to taste.

QUALITY GROUND CORN IS THE KEY

TITLE:

POPCORN GRITS WITH CARAMELIZED MUSHROOMS

SERVES:

4 to 6

NOTES / INGREDIENTS / METHOD:

Who doesn't love buttered popcorn? We wanted to infuse the grits with the flavor of popcorn to create something new and exciting. Corn is corn at the end of the day, so we brought together two ways of enjoying it. We created a super-flavorful popcorn liquid to serve as the base, and then we topped the cooked grits with freshly popped kernels, mushrooms, and Parmesan. The combination is irresistible and impressive for a dinner party.

8 ounces various mushrooms
  (such as cremini, oyster,
  shiitake, chanterelle, white),
  sliced ¼ inch thick
Extra-virgin olive oil
Kosher salt
Freshly ground black pepper
4 tablespoons grapeseed or
  vegetable oil, for frying
⅓ cup popcorn kernels

1 quart whole milk
½ teaspoon truffle oil
6 thyme sprigs
2 garlic cloves, smashed
¾ cup yellow cornmeal
1½ tablespoons unsalted butter
¼ cup freshly grated Parmesan
  cheese, plus more for garnish
¼ bunch of chives, trimmed to
  2-inch *batons*

Preheat the oven to 450°F. Put the mushrooms in one layer on a sheet pan and drizzle with a little olive oil. Season with salt and pepper. Roast for 15 minutes, until the mushrooms are golden brown.

Heat the grapeseed oil in a large pot over medium-high heat. Add the popcorn kernels and cover. Soon, you'll hear the popcorn pop. Shake the pot occasionally as it pops. Once the popping slows to once every couple of seconds, take the pot off the heat; it will be very hot. Remove ½ cup of the popped corn and set aside. Add the milk, ¾ cup water, truffle oil, thyme sprigs, and garlic to the pot. Bring the mixture to a boil, then reduce to a low simmer and cook for 10 minutes. Remove the herb sprigs from the milk mixture and pour the mixture into a blender. Process until smooth, then strain.

INFUSE THE MILK

Transfer the strained milk mixture to a medium saucepan over medium heat, and bring to a boil. "Rain in" the cornmeal, whisking so that it doesn't clump. Turn the heat down to a simmer and cook, stirring continuously so that the corn doesn't burn on the bottom of the pot. The cornmeal will absorb the liquid in about 15 minutes. If you'd like the grits smoother, cook them longer, adding water or milk if they get too thick. Finish by stirring in the butter, ¼ cup Parmesan, and salt and pepper to taste.

Place the grits in a serving dish. Top with the roasted mushrooms, reserved popcorn, chive *batons*, and additional Parmesan. Serve immediately.

TRUFFLE POPCORN + GRITS = A GREAT DINNER

FRESH CORN POBLANO "GRITS"

NOTES / INGREDIENTS / METHOD:

It was the height of summer in California when we were testing grits recipes, and fresh corn was abundant at farmers' markets. We wanted to take advantage of the season, so we developed a "grits" dish that relies entirely on fresh corn—there is no cornmeal in this recipe. In traditional grits, you are actually rehydrating ground dried meal corn, so we figured we could start with fresh sweet corn and skip the grinding and rehydrating steps. This recipe relies on the taste of the corn rather than on the cream or butter to make it sing—it is entirely vegan, in fact. We made a stock using the cobs, too, so as to take advantage of the entire vegetable. This is one of our favorite discoveries while testing recipes for this book.

4 ears of corn	**1 poblano pepper**
1 large onion	**Extra-virgin olive oil**
3 bay leaves	**Kosher salt**
8 thyme sprigs	**Cilantro sprigs**
4 garlic cloves	**Coarse sea salt**
1 tablespoon black peppercorns	**Smoked olive oil (optional)**

REMOVE THE KERNELS

Preheat the oven to 425°F. Pull back the husks from the corn to expose about 3 inches of the cob. Place the corn on a sheet pan. Quarter the onion, and add to the sheet pan. Roast about 20 minutes, until the husks start to brown and the corn is just cooked.

Remove the husks and silks. Stand each cob on its end in another sheet pan, and holding the top, slice downward along the cob to remove the kernels. (Doing this over a sheet pan catches the kernels for you.) Set the kernels aside. Place the cobs, roasted onion, the bay leaves, thyme sprigs, garlic, and peppercorns in a pot and cover with water. (If you need to, snap the cobs in half to fit into the pot.) Bring to a boil, then lower the heat to a gentle simmer for 45 minutes to make a stock.

Place half of the kernels in a blender with one ladle of the developing stock, and puree until smooth. Now you have fresh corn "grits."

Transfer the remaining kernels to a cutting board. Take the seeds out of the poblano pepper, and chop the pepper to roughly the same size as the corn kernels. Then chop the pepper and corn together until very fine. Coat a large sauté pan with some olive oil and set over medium-high heat. Add the chopped corn mixture to the pan and cook for 3 to 5 minutes, just to sweat and soften. Scoop up some of the roasted onion pieces from the stock and add to the corn mixture. Pour in the fresh corn "grits" and 1 cup of the corn stock. Cook for another 5 minutes or so, until the grits thicken to a porridge-like consistency. If they are too thick, add more stock; if too thin, cook them a bit longer. Season with salt.

Place the grits in a serving dish, and garnish with a few segments of the roasted onion from the stock along with a few cilantro sprigs, a sprinkle of coarse sea salt, and a drizzle of smoked or extra-virgin olive oil.

THE ULTIMATE
SUMMER
SIDE DISH

EXTRA-LIGHT CORNBREAD

FRY THE CORNMEAL IN BACON FAT

POUR THE BATTER INTO THE CRISP CORNMEAL

NOTES / INGREDIENTS / METHOD:

A good piece of cornbread should be light and irresistible, but so many times it is dense and tastes like it came out of a box. In the Test Kitchen, we reengineered the idea so it became a hybrid of cornbread and gougère (French cheese puff). We riffed on the idea of making a popover; instead of leavening agents, we relied on beaten eggs. In short, there's no reason you can't rethink whatever tradition has put on your table to make it new and modern; that is one of the fun parts of being in the Test Kitchen. Use freshly milled organic cornmeal if you can; it will make a huge difference in the final product.

⅓ cup plus 4 tablespoons yellow cornmeal
⅓ cup all-purpose flour
⅛ teaspoon kosher salt
¼ cup sugar
¾ cup (1½ sticks) unsalted butter

¾ cup buttermilk
6 large eggs
4 strips of bacon (or 2 tablespoons canola oil, if preferred)
2 teaspoons chopped chives

Preheat the oven to 375°F.

Grind the ⅓ cup cornmeal in a food processor or blender until it is very fine, like talcum powder. In a mixing bowl, combine the ground cornmeal with the flour, salt, and sugar.

Melt the butter in a medium saucepan with the buttermilk and ¾ cup of water, and bring the mixture to a simmer. Add the dry ingredients and stir to combine.

Transfer the batter to a stand mixer, and beat with the whip attachment at medium-low speed to cool the batter. Continue mixing for 4 or 5 minutes, until the batter comes together and becomes shiny, like *pâte à choux.* Add the eggs one at a time, alternating with 3 tablespoons coarse cornmeal for texture.

In a medium cast-iron skillet, cook the bacon over medium heat until crisp. (If using canola oil, skip this step and heat the canola oil in the skillet.) Drain the bacon on a paper towel and reserve for a garnish. Add the remaining 1 tablespoon coarse cornmeal to the hot fat and fry until fragrant, about a minute. Pour the batter into the skillet and bake for 30 to 35 minutes, until the edges are golden brown and pull away from the skillet. Garnish with the reserved bacon and chopped chives.

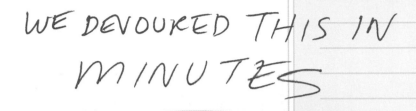

WE DEVOURED THIS IN
MINUTES

FRONION FAILS

One of the best ways to develop a new recipe is to read up on how people have done it before and then find all the ways you wish it could be different. For our Fronion Rings (page 252), we sampled some onion-ring game changers from the past:

- **Beer batter/tempura hybrid:** Since warm water is really good at activating gluten, making batters elastic and structured, the method for tempura uses ice-cold water to help keep the mix light and lacy. And beer batter recipes take advantage of the carbonation in beer to further lighten the batter. So we combined the two to see what would happen. The carbohydrates in the beer converted to sugar and turned the crust dark before the onion cooked or the batter got crispy, so this version did not make the cut—but we liked how carbonated water "puffed" the batter.

- **Soda water:** We used soda water instead of beer. The bigger bubbles in the soda water made for crunchier results than the beer batter, but they did not taste like anything new. We felt that we had tasted this version of an onion ring before, so we thought we could change the flavor profile a bit.

- **Vodka:** We used vodka as the liquid, another popular technique because alcohol evaporates more quickly than water and has the added benefit of not developing the gluten the way water does. In theory this creates lighter, crispier onion rings, but for us that didn't hold up, as the batter got very lacy instead of forming a solid crust. But one time we used potato starch, and it tasted a little like a french fry, inspiring us to think of the french fry–coated Fronion that resulted. The laciness of the batter meant that the batter wasn't clinging to the onion enough, but a thickener like xanthan gum would help it hold on to the rings and a little baking powder would give it more "puff."

Even though each of these techniques left something to be desired, they all made a contribution and we pulled them all together—with our own twist, of course.

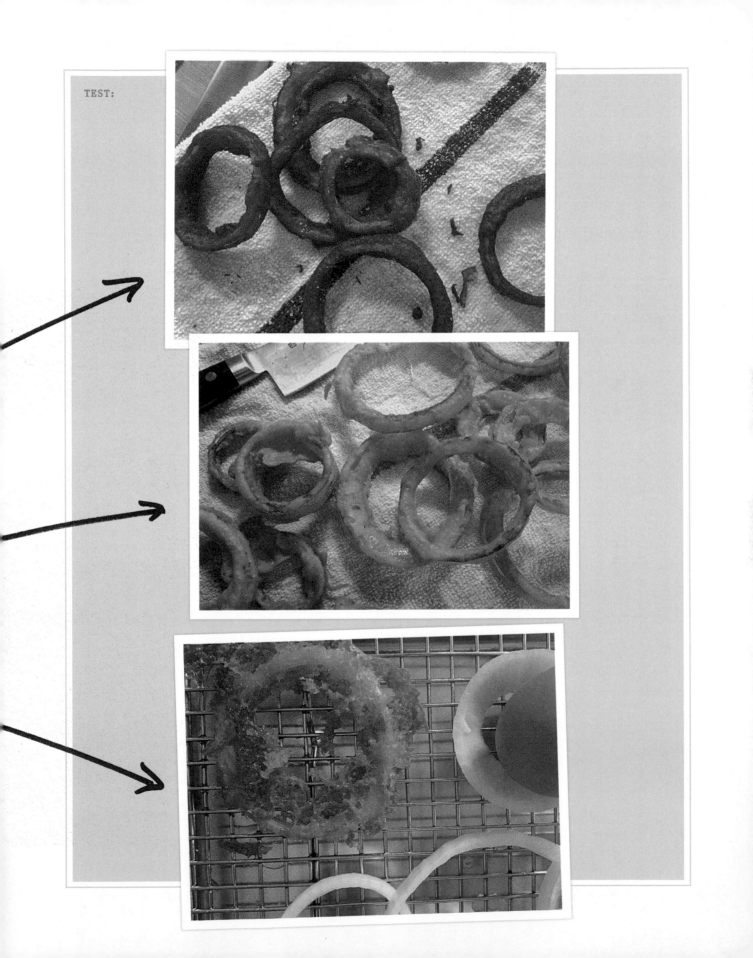

FRONION RINGS

4 to 6

PAT THE ONIONS
DRY BEFORE
DREDGING

NOTES / INGREDIENTS / METHOD:

French fries or onion rings? It's a classic fast-food conundrum, but while chatting in the Test Kitchen during our onion ring testing, we realized we were forcing a choice that didn't have to be made: we coated an onion ring with a french fry. The stabilizer here is xanthan gum, a natural product; it thickens a liquid without adding flavor. It is also a common ingredient in gluten-free baking, as it can replicate the binding effect of gluten. Using rice flour instead of all-purpose gives a light, super-crispy batter.

2 large Spanish onions
¼ cup salt
¼ cup sugar
1 tablespoon white vinegar
4½ cups rice flour
1 teaspoon baking powder

1 quart cold soda water
1 teaspoon xanthan gum
2 cups frozen french fries
Grapeseed or canola oil, for frying
Kosher salt

FRY UNTIL
HONEY GOLDEN

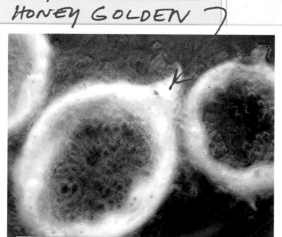

Cut the onions into 1-inch-thick slices, and break into rings with your hands. In a large bowl, stir together the salt, sugar, vinegar, and 1 quart of water (not the soda water). Add the onions to the brine, and let soak for 10 to 15 minutes. The brine will impart flavor and partially soften the onions.

Mix 3 cups of the rice flour and baking powder in a bowl. Pour the soda water into a blender, turn it on, and add the xanthan gum; the xanthan gum will thicken, and will continue to thicken once the blender blade stops moving. Pour the soda water mixture into the dry ingredients and stir. Pour the batter back into the blender, add the frozen french fries, and puree until smooth. Transfer the batter to a large bowl.

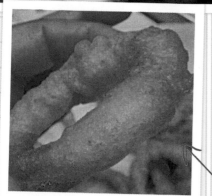

Pour 4 inches of grapeseed oil into a large pot with several inches of clearance. Heat over medium-high heat to 350°F. Remove the onions from the brine and pat dry with a clean towel. Dredge the onions in the remaining 1½ cups rice flour, then dip in the batter until they are well coated. Fry the onion rings in the oil, a few at a time, for 2 to 3 minutes, or until they are a honey-golden brown, then drain on a paper towel–lined sheet tray. Sprinkle with salt and serve immediately.

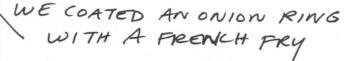

WE COATED AN ONION RING
WITH A FRENCH FRY

INDEX

Note: Page references in *italics* refer to photographs of finished recipes.

Aioli
Curry Court-Bouillon, 218–19, *219*
Herb, 152–53, *153*
Roasted Garlic, 190
Almond Milk Brine, 150, *150*

Anchovy(ies)
Caesar Dressing, 225
Caesar Salad "Deviled Eggs," *104,* 104–5
Green Goddess Shreds, 20, *20*
-Parmesan Potato Croutons, Caesar Salad with, 223–25, *224*

Appetizers and snacks
Apricot-Thyme Preserves, 53, *53*
Cheddar–Black Pepper Crackers, 52, *53*
Classic Deviled Eggs, 102–3, *102–3*
Cranberry "Salami," *84,* 85
Fig-Hazelnut Fruit "Salami," 54, *55*
French Onion Arancini, 208–9, *209*
Fresh Tortilla Chips and Roasted Tomato–Pepper Salsa, 182, *183*
Fried Black-Eyed Peas, 241, *241*
Garlic-Herb Potato Chips, *196,* 197–98
Oysters Rockefeller with Double-Creamed Spinach, *234,* 234–35
Seared and Chopped Chicken Liver Toast, 72–73, *73*
Super-Light Cheese Straws, 50–51, *51*
Sweet and Spicy Prosciutto-Ricotta Toasts, 58, *59*

Apple(s)
Brussels Sprouts, and Bacon, Roasted, Pork Chops with, 160, *160*
Caramelized, Mustard, 166, *166*
Kale Waldorf Chicken Salad, *74,* 75
Pecan Muffins, 112

Apricot
-Fennel Salad and Creamed Kale, Pork Chops with, *154,* 155
-Thyme Preserves, 53, *53*
Arancini, French Onion, 208–9, *209*
Artichokes with Curry Court-Bouillon Aioli, 218–19, *219*

Avocado(s)
Eggs Benedict, California, 98, *99*
Guacamole, 180, *181*
-Meatloaf Sandwich, 40

Bacon
Apple, and Brussels Sprouts, Roasted, Pork Chops with, 160, *160*
Caramelized Brussels Sprouts with Pancetta, 228, *229*
Carbonara with Creamy Scrambled Eggs, 134–35, *135*
The Egg-Roll Omelet, 94–95, *95*
Extra-Light Cornbread, 248, *249*
Grilled Cheese, 47
House-Smoked, 168–69, *169*
Loaded Iceberg Wedge Salad, 226, *227*
Oysters Rockefeller with Double-Creamed Spinach, *234,* 234–35
Risotto Carbonara, *204,* 205
Waffles, 115

Banana(s)
Bran Muffins, 112
Caramelized, and Herb Aioli, Pork Chops with, 152–53, *153*
Roasted, Sour Cream, Roasted Sweet Potatoes with, 88–89, *89*
Thai Chicken Salad, *70,* 70–71
Waffles, 115

Bean(s)
Baked, California, 21, *21*
Black-Eyed Pea and Charred Vegetable Chili, *238,* 238–40
Classic Black-Eyed Peas with Ham Hock, 236, *237*
Fried Black-Eyed Peas, 241, *241*
Green, Poutine, 86–87, *87*
Salad Niçoise Carpaccio, 220–21, *221*
Tomato and Black-Eyed Pea Salad, 242, *242*

Beef. *See also* Veal
The Burger, *34,* 35–36
Gnocchi Bolognese, 131, *131*
Meatloaf with Tomato Relish, *38,* 38–39
One-Pan Lasagna, 144–46, *145*
Slow-Cooked Bolognese Sauce, 132–33, *133*
Spaghetti and Meatballs, 138–39, *139*

Berry(ies)
Burst, Lemon Cake with, 117
Cranberry "Salami," *84,* 85
Icebox Strawberry-Ricotta Cheesecake Bombe, *60,* 61–62
Pancakes, 113
Updated Cranberry Sauce with Celery-Walnut Salad, 82, *83*

Black-Eyed Pea(s)
and Charred Vegetable Chili, *238,* 238–40
Classic, with Ham Hock, 236, *237*
Fried, 241, *241*
and Tomato Salad, 242, *242*
Bourbon Peach Cobbler, 23–24, *24*
Bran Muffins, Banana, 112
Bread-and-Butter Pickles and Cheese, 22, *22*

Breads. *See also* Muffins
Extra-Light Cornbread, 248, *249*
Modern Burger Buns, 28–29, *29*
Parker House Rolls with Parsley-Garlic Butter, *18,* 18–19
Seared and Chopped Chicken Liver Toast, 72–73, *73*
Summer Panzanella, 216–17, *217*
Sweet and Spicy Prosciutto-Ricotta Toasts, 58, *59*
Test Kitchen Stuffing, 90
Brine, Almond Milk, 150, *150*

Brussels Sprouts
Apple, and Bacon, Roasted, Pork Chops with, 160, *160*
Caramelized, with Pancetta, 228, *229*
Burger Buns, Modern, 28–29, *29*
Burger Goop, 36
The Burger, *34,* 35–36
Butter, Parsley-Garlic, 19
Buttermilk-Herb Dressing, 76
Butterscotch Pancakes, 113

Caesar Dressing, 225
Caesar Salad "Deviled Eggs," *104,* 104–5
Caesar Salad with Anchovy-Parmesan Potato Croutons, 223–25, *224*

Cakes, 116, *116*
Coffee, 117
Five-in-One Mix for, 111
Icebox Strawberry-Ricotta Cheesecake Bombe, *60,* 61–62
Lemon, with Burst Berries, 117
Pineapple Upside-Down, 117

Carrot(s)
Hibiscus Escabeche, 186, *186*
Triple-, Risotto, 202–3, *203*

Celery
Kale Waldorf Chicken Salad, *74,* 75
-Walnut Salad, Updated Cranberry Sauce with, 82, *83*

Cheese
and Bread-and-Butter Pickles, 22, *22*
Caesar Salad "Deviled Eggs," *104,* 104–5
Caesar Salad with Anchovy-Parmesan Potato Croutons, 223–25, *224*
California Avocado Eggs Benedict, 98, *99*
Carbonara with Creamy Scrambled Eggs, 134–35, *135*
Cheddar–Black Pepper Crackers, 52, *53*
The Egg-Roll Omelet, 94–95, *95*
French Onion Arancini, 208–9, *209*
Gnocchi Pomodoro, 130, *130*
Green Bean Poutine, 86–87, *87*
Grilled, Bacon, 47
Grilled, Modern, 46–47, *47*

Cheese (*continued*)
Grilled, Mushroom, 47
Homemade Fresh Ricotta, 57, *57*
Icebox Strawberry-Ricotta
Cheesecake Bombe, *60,* 61–62
Kale Waldorf Chicken Salad, *74,* 75
Lemon-Ricotta Pancakes, 113
Loaded Iceberg Wedge Salad, 226, *227*
One-Pan Lasagna, 144–46, *145*
Roasted and Grilled Mexican Corn,
184, 184–85
Spinach-Ricotta Tortellini, 136–37, *137*
Straws, Super-Light, 50–51, *51*
Stretchy Mac and, *48,* 49
Sweet and Spicy Prosciutto-Ricotta
Toasts, 58, *59*
Cheesecake Bombe, Icebox
Strawberry-Ricotta, *60,* 61–62
Chicken
Fried, Wayfare Tavern's, 65–67, *67*
Liver, Seared and Chopped, Toast,
72–73, *73*
One-Pan Lasagna, 144–46, *145*
Paella Risotto, *206,* 206–7
Roast, Super-Crisp, *68,* 69
Salad, Kale Waldorf, *74,* 75
Salad, Thai, *70,* 70–71
Chiles
California Baked Beans, 21, *21*
Chile Powder, 241
Fresh Corn Poblano "Grits," 246–47,
247
Guacamole, 180, *181*
Hibiscus Escabeche, 186, *186*
Roasted Sweet Potatoes with
Roasted Banana Sour Cream,
88–89, *89*
Roasted Tomato–Pepper Salsa,
182–83, *183*
Sweet and Spicy Prosciutto-Ricotta
Toasts, 58, *59*
Tomatillo Salsa Verde, *175,* 178
Chili, Black-Eyed Pea and Charred
Vegetable, *238,* 238–40
Chile Powder, 241
Chocolate
Chip Cookies, 120
Chip Pancakes, 113
Soufflés, Infallible, *106,* 106–7
Cilantro
Guacamole, 180, *181*
Roasted Tomato–Pepper Salsa,
182–83, *183*
Tomatillo Salsa Verde, *175,* 178
Cobbler, Bourbon Peach, 23–24, *24*
Coffee Cake, 117
Cookies, 118–19, *120*
Chocolate Chip, 120
Five-in-One Mix for, 111
Oatmeal, 120
Peanut Butter, 120

Corn
Fresh, Poblano "Grits," 246–47, *247*
Roasted and Grilled Mexican, *184,*
184–85
Summer Panzanella, 216–17, *217*
Cornbread, Extra-Light, 248, *249*
Cornbread Muffins, 112
Cornmeal
Cornbread Muffins, 112
Creamy Carolina Grits, 243, *243*
Extra-Light Cornbread, 248, *249*
Polenta Gnocchi, *128,* 128–29
Crackers, Cheddar–Black Pepper, 52,
53
Cranberry
"Salami," *84,* 85
Sauce, Updated, with Celery-Walnut
Salad, 82, *83*
Cucumbers
Bread-and-Butter Pickles and
Cheese, 22, *22*
Summer Panzanella, 216–17, *217*

Desserts
Bourbon Peach Cobbler, 23–24, *24*
Cake, 116, *116*
Chocolate Chip Cookies, 120
Cookies, 118–19, *120*
Icebox Strawberry-Ricotta
Cheesecake Bombe, *60,* 61–62
Infallible Chocolate Soufflés, *106,*
106–7
Infallible Raspberry Soufflé, 107
Lemon Cake with Burst Berries, 117
Oatmeal Cookies, 120
Peanut Butter Cookies, 120
Pineapple Upside-Down Cake, 117
Deviled Eggs, Classic, 102–3, *102–3*
"Deviled Eggs," Caesar Salad, *104,*
104–5
Dips. *See also* Salsa
Curry Court-Bouillon Aioli, 218–19,
219
Guacamole, 180, *181*
Herb Aioli, 152–53, *153*
Roasted Garlic Aioli, 190
Dressings
Buttermilk-Herb, 76
Caesar, 225
Tuna Confit, 222

Eggs
Benedict, California Avocado, 98, *99*
Creamy Scrambled, Carbonara with,
134–35, *135*
Deviled, Classic, 102–3, *102–3*
"Deviled," Caesar Salad, *104,* 104–5
The Egg-Roll Omelet, 94–95, *95*
Infallible Chocolate Soufflés, *106,*
106–7
Infallible Raspberry Soufflé, 107

Marge's Potato Salad, *194,* 194–95
Perfect Steamed "Boiled," 101, *101*
Poached, No-Sweat, 96, *96*
Risotto Carbonara, *204,* 205
Salad Niçoise Carpaccio, 220–21, *221*
Scrambled, Super-Creamy, 93, *93*
Escabeche, Hibiscus, 186, *186*

Fennel
-Apricot Salad and Creamed Kale,
Pork Chops with, *154,* 155
Side Salad for Meatloaf, *38,* 39–40
Slow-Roasted Ham "Porchetta," *163,*
163–64
Fig(s)
-Hazelnut Fruit "Salami," 54, *55*
Sweet and Spicy Prosciutto-Ricotta
Toasts, 58, *59*
Fish. *See* Anchovy(ies); Shellfish; Tuna
Five-in-One Mix, 111
French Fries with Roasted Garlic Aioli,
189–90, *191*
Fronion Rings, 252, *252*

Garlic
-Herb Potato Chips, *196,* 197–98
-Parsley Butter, 19
Roasted, Aioli, 190
Gnocchi
Bolognese, 131, *131*
Polenta, *128,* 128–29
Pomodoro, 130, *130*
Grains. *See also* Cornmeal; Rice
Banana Bran Muffins, 112
Creamy Carolina Grits, 243, *243*
Oatmeal Cookies, 120
Popcorn Grits with Caramelized
Mushrooms, 244–45, *245*
Green Bean(s)
Poutine, 86–87, *87*
Salad Niçoise Carpaccio, 220–21, *221*
Greens. *See also* Lettuce; Spinach
Kale Waldorf Chicken Salad, *74,* 75
Pork Chops with Creamed Kale and
Fennel-Apricot Salad, *154,* 155
Side Salad for Meatloaf, *38,* 39–40
Slow-Roasted Ham "Porchetta," *163,*
163–64
Grits
Creamy Carolina, 243, *243*
Popcorn, with Caramelized
Mushrooms, 244–45, *245*
"Grits," Fresh Corn Poblano, 246–47,
247
Guacamole, 180, *181*

Ham
Hock, Classic Black-Eyed Peas with,
236, *237*
"Porchetta," Slow-Roasted, *163,*
163–64

Smoke-Roasted Hawaiian, *170,*
171–72
Sweet and Spicy Prosciutto-Ricotta
Toasts, 58, *59*
Hazelnut-Fig Fruit "Salami," 54, *55*
Herb(s). *See also specific herbs*
Aioli, 152–53, *153*
-Buttermilk Dressing, 76
-Garlic Potato Chips, *196,* 197–98
Herbed Pomodoro Sauce, 141, *141*
-Roasted Wild Mushrooms with Red
Wine and Cream, *230,* 230–31
Hibiscus Escabeche, 186, *186*
Hollandaise, Three-Minute Blender,
97, *97*
Horchata-Tofu "Sour Cream," 239–40

Kale
Creamed, and Fennel-Apricot Salad,
Pork Chops with, *154,* 155
Waldorf Chicken Salad, *74,* 75

Lasagna
Fresh, 124
One-Pan, 144–46, *145*
Lemon
Cake with Burst Berries, 117
-Ricotta Pancakes, 113
Lettuce
Caesar Salad "Deviled Eggs," *104,*
104–5
Caesar Salad with Anchovy-
Parmesan Potato Croutons,
223–25, *224*
Green Goddess Shreds, 20, *20*
Loaded Iceberg Wedge Salad, 226,
227
Liver, Chicken, Seared and Chopped,
Toast, 72–73, *73*

Meatballs, Spaghetti and, 138–39, *139*
Meatloaf
-Avocado Sandwich, 40
with Tomato Relish, *38,* 38–39
Muffins, 112, *112*
Apple Pecan, 112
Banana Bran, 112
Cornbread, 112
Five-in-One Mix for, 111
Mushroom(s)
Caramelized, Popcorn Grits with,
244–45, *245*
The Egg-Roll Omelet, 94–95, *95*
Green Bean Poutine, 86–87, *87*
Grilled Cheese, 47
Risotto Carbonara, *204,* 205
Wild, Herb-Roasted, with Red Wine
and Cream, *230,* 230–31
Mustard
Barbecue Sauce, Carolina, 17
Caramelized Apple, 166, *166*

Nuts. *See also* Walnut(s)
Apple Pecan Muffins, 112
Fig-Hazelnut Fruit "Salami," 54, *55*

Oatmeal Cookies, 120
Olive(s)
Black, Tapenade, Seared Summer
Squash, and Tomato, Pork Chops
with, 156, *157*
Salad Niçoise Carpaccio, 220–21, *221*
Summer Panzanella, 216–17, *217*
Omelet, The Egg-Roll, 94–95, *95*
Onion(s)
French, Arancini, 208–9, *209*
Fried, Double-Creamed Spinach
with, 232–33, *233*
Fronion Rings, 252, *252*
Pork Chops with Caramelized
Bananas and Herb Aioli, 152–53,
153
Oysters Rockefeller with Double-
Creamed Spinach, *234,* 234–35

Paella Risotto, *206,* 206–7
Pancakes, 113, *113*
Berry, 113
Butterscotch, 113
Chocolate Chip, 113
Five-in-One Mix for, 111
Lemon-Ricotta, 113
Pancetta
Risotto Carbonara, *204,* 205
Panzanella, Summer, 216–17, *217*
Pappardelle, Fresh, 124
Parker House Rolls with Parsley-Garlic
Butter, *18,* 18–19
Parsley-Garlic Butter, 19
Pasta
Carbonara with Creamy Scrambled
Eggs, 134–35, *135*
Fresh, 123–24, *125*
Gnocchi Bolognese, 131, *131*
Gnocchi Pomodoro, 130, *130*
Lasagna, 124
One-Pan Lasagna, 144–46, *145*
Pappardelle, 124
Polenta Gnocchi, *128,* 128–29
Ravioli, 124
Shrimp and Spam Lo Mein, 173–74
Spaghetti, 124
Spaghetti and Meatballs, 138–39, *139*
Spaghetti with Summer Squash and
Pine Nuts, *142,* 142–43
Spinach-Ricotta Tortellini, 136–37,
137
Stretchy Mac and Cheese, *48,* 49
Stuffed, 124
Tortellini, 124
Peach(es)
Cobbler, Bourbon, 23–24, *24*
Summer Panzanella, 216–17, *217*

Peanut Butter Cookies, 120
Pecan Apple Muffins, 112
Peppers. *See also* Chiles
Black-Eyed Pea and Charred
Vegetable Chili, 238, 238–40
Tomato Relish, 38–39
Pickles, Bread-and-Butter, and Cheese,
22, *22*
Pineapple
Cranberry "Salami," *84,* 85
Shrimp and Spam Lo Mein, 173–74
Smoke-Roasted Hawaiian Ham, *170,*
171–72
Updated Cranberry Sauce with
Celery-Walnut Salad, 82, *83*
Upside-Down Cake, 117
Polenta Gnocchi, *128,* 128–29
Popcorn Grits with Caramelized
Mushrooms, 244–45, *245*
Pork. *See also* Bacon; Ham; Sausages
Carnitas Tacos with Tomatillo Salsa
Verde, *175,* 177–78
Chops, Seared Brined, 151, *151*
Chops with Caramelized Bananas
and Herb Aioli, 152–53, *153*
Chops with Creamed Kale and
Fennel-Apricot Salad, *154,* 155
Chops with Roasted Apple, Brussels
Sprouts, and Bacon, 160, *160*
Chops with Seared Summer Squash,
Tomato, and Black Olive Tapenade,
156, *157*
Gnocchi Bolognese, 131, *131*
Meatloaf with Tomato Relish, *38,*
38–39
Schnitzel with Sage and Capers, *158,*
158–59
Shoulder or St. Louis Ribs, Crispy
Smoked, *15,* 15–16
Slow-Cooked Bolognese Sauce,
132–33, *133*
Spaghetti and Meatballs, 138–39,
139
Potato(es)
Chips, Garlic-Herb, *196,* 197–98
Croutons, Anchovy-Parmesan,
Caesar Salad with, 223–25, *224*
French Fries with Roasted Garlic
Aioli, 189–90, *191*
Fronion Rings, 252, *252*
Mashed, Extra Potato-y, 192, *193*
Salad, Marge's, *194,* 194–95
Salad Niçoise Carpaccio, 220–21, *221*
Sweet, Roasted, with Roasted
Banana Sour Cream, 88–89, *89*
Poultry. *See* Chicken; Turkey
Poutine, Green Bean, 86–87, *87*
Preserves, Apricot-Thyme, 53, *53*
Prosciutto-Ricotta Toasts, Sweet and
Spicy, 58, *59*
Pumpkin Waffles, 115

Raspberry Soufflé, Infallible, 107
Ravioli, Fresh, 124
Relish, Tomato, 38–39
Rice
    French Onion Arancini, 208–9, *209*
    Paella Risotto, *206,* 206–7
    Risotto Carbonara, *204,* 205
    "Shrimp and Grits" Risotto, 210–12, *211*
    Time-Saver Risotto, *199,* 201
    Tofu-Horchata "Sour Cream," 239–40
    Triple-Carrot Risotto, 202–3, *203*
Risotto
    Carbonara, *204,* 205
    Paella, *206,* 206–7
    "Shrimp and Grits," 210–12, *211*
    Time-Saver, *199,* 201
    Triple-Carrot, 202–3, *203*
Rolls, Parker House, with Parsley-Garlic Butter, *18,* 18–19
Rub, California Dry, 17

Salads
    Caesar, "Deviled Eggs," *104,* 104–5
    Caesar, with Anchovy-Parmesan Potato Croutons, 223–25, *224*
    Celery-Walnut, Updated Cranberry Sauce with, 82, *83*
    Chicken, Thai, *70,* 70–71
    Green Goddess Shreds, 20, *20*
    Kale Waldorf Chicken, *74,* 75
    Loaded Iceberg Wedge, 226, *227*
    Potato, Marge's, *194,* 194–95
    Salad Niçoise Carpaccio, 220–21, *221*
    Side, for Meatloaf, *38,* 39–40
    Summer Panzanella, 216–17, *217*
    Tomato and Black-Eyed Pea, 242, *242*
"Salami," Cranberry, *84,* 85
"Salami," Fig-Hazelnut Fruit, 54, *55*
Salsa
    Roasted Tomato–Pepper, 182–83, *183*
    Tomatillo, Verde, *175,* 178
Sandwiches
    Bacon Grilled Cheese, 47
    Meatloaf-Avocado, 40
    Modern Grilled Cheese, 46–47, *47*
    Mushroom Grilled Cheese, 47
Sauces. *See also* Salsa
    Barbecue, Carolina Mustard, 17
    Bolognese, Slow-Cooked, 132–33, *133*
    Burger Goop, 36
    Curry Court-Bouillon Aioli, 218–19, *219*
    Herb Aioli, 152–53, *153*
    Pomodoro, Herbed, 141, *141*
    Roasted Garlic Aioli, 190
    Thanksgiving, 80, *80*
    Thanksgiving, Vegetarian, 81
    Three-Minute Blender Hollandaise, 97, *97*

Updated Cranberry, with Celery-Walnut Salad, 82, *83*
Sausages
    Paella Risotto, *206,* 206–7
    "Shrimp and Grits" Risotto, 210–12, *211*
    Test Kitchen Stuffing, 90
Shellfish
    Oysters Rockefeller with Double-Creamed Spinach, *234,* 234–35
    Paella Risotto, *206,* 206–7
    "Shrimp and Grits" Risotto, 210–12, *211*
    Shrimp and Spam Lo Mein, 173–74
Shrimp
    "and Grits" Risotto, 210–12, *211*
    Paella Risotto, *206,* 206–7
    and Spam Lo Mein, 173–74
Soufflés
    Infallible Chocolate, *106,* 106–7
    Infallible Raspberry, 107
"Sour Cream," Tofu-Horchata, 239–40
Spaghetti
    Fresh, 124
    and Meatballs, 138–39, *139*
    with Summer Squash and Pine Nuts, *142,* 142–43
Spam
    and Shrimp Lo Mein, 173–74
    Smoke-Roasted Hawaiian Ham, *170,* 171–72
Spice blends
    California Dry Rub, 17
    Chile Powder, 241
Spinach
    Double-Creamed, Oysters Rockefeller with, *234,* 234–35
    Double-Creamed, with Fried Onions, 232–33, *233*
    The Egg-Roll Omelet, 94–95, *95*
    One-Pan Lasagna, 144–46, *145*
    -Ricotta Tortellini, 136–37, *137*
Squash
    Pumpkin Waffles, 115
    Summer, and Pine Nuts, Spaghetti with, *142,* 142–43
    Summer, Seared, Tomato, and Black Olive Tapenade, Pork Chops with, 156, *157*
Strawberry-Ricotta Cheesecake Bombe, Icebox, *60,* 61–62
Stuffing, Test Kitchen, 90
Sweet Potatoes, Roasted, with Roasted Banana Sour Cream, 88–89, *89*

Tacos, Pork Carnitas, with Tomatillo Salsa Verde, *175,* 177–78
Tofu-Horchata "Sour Cream," 239–40
Tomatillo Salsa Verde, *175,* 178
Tomato(es)
    and Black-Eyed Pea Salad, 242, *242*

Gnocchi Pomodoro, 130, *130*
Herbed Pomodoro Sauce, 141, *141*
Loaded Iceberg Wedge Salad, 226, *227*
One-Pan Lasagna, 144–46, *145*
Relish, 38–39
Roasted, –Pepper Salsa, 182–83, *183*
Salad Niçoise Carpaccio, 220–21, *221*
Seared Summer Squash, and Black Olive Tapenade, Pork Chops with, 156, *157*
Slow-Cooked Bolognese Sauce, 132–33, *133*
Summer Panzanella, 216–17, *217*
Tortellini
    Fresh, 124
    Spinach-Ricotta, 136–37, *137*
Tortilla(s)
    Chips, Fresh, and Roasted Tomato–Pepper Salsa, 182, *183*
    Pork Carnitas Tacos with Tomatillo Salsa Verde, *175,* 177–78
Tuna
    Confit Dressing, 222
    Salad Niçoise Carpaccio, 220–21, *221*
Turkey
    One-Pan Lasagna, 144–46, *145*
    Roast, Super-Fast, 78–79, *79*
Turnip Puree, 167, *167*

Veal
    Gnocchi Bolognese, 131, *131*
    Slow-Cooked Bolognese Sauce, 132–33, *133*
    Spaghetti and Meatballs, 138–39, *139*
Vegetable(s). *See also specific vegetables*
    Charred, and Black-Eyed Pea Chili, *238,* 238–40
    Summer Panzanella, 216–17, *217*

Waffles, *114,* 115
    Bacon, 115
    Banana, 115
    Five-in-One Mix for, 111
    Pumpkin, 115
Walnut(s)
    -Celery Salad, Updated Cranberry Sauce with, 82, *83*
    Cranberry "Salami," *84,* 85
    Kale Waldorf Chicken Salad, *74,* 75
    Triple-Carrot Risotto, 202–3, *203*

Zucchini
    Pork Chops with Seared Summer Squash, Tomato, and Black Olive Tapenade, 156, *157*
    Spaghetti with Summer Squash and Pine Nuts, *142,* 142–43